# ABOUT OUR BOYS

LUCINDA NEALL has a son, a stepson and a stepdaughter, and has worked with young people in a voluntary capacity most of her life. She set up the Leighton Buzzard Youth Forum and runs her local youth club.

She earns her living working with businesses and schools on teambuilding, motivation and communication skills. Since the publication of her first book, *Bringing the Best out in Boys – Communication Strategies for Teachers,* she has spent a lot of time working with teachers and parents on how to set boys up to succeed.

## ALSO BY LUCINDA NEALL

*Bringing the Best out in Boys – Communication Strategies for Teachers*

'Will certainly make teachers think, and be alert to what's different about teaching boys, and how to make this more of a pleasure.'
Steve Biddulph, author of *Manhood* and *Raising Boys*

'Lucinda Neall's wise book ... is one of the most interesting accounts available of an over-familiar issue, distinguished by its practical approach.'
*Times Educational Supplement*

'This book makes a notable contribution because it tries to tackle the issues in a positive way, without reducing opportunities for girls. It emphasises positive steps that teachers can take.'
Ted Wragg

Lucinda Neall

# ABOUT OUR BOYS

## A practical guide to bringing out the best in boys

| | |
|---|---|
| **WARRINGTON BOROUGH COUNCIL** | |
| | |
| **Askews** | 08-Dec-2008 |
| | |
| | |

Neall Scott Partnership

*About Our Boys: A Practical Guide to Bringing out the Best in Boys*
copyright © 2007 Lucinda Neall

Published by the Neall Scott Partnership Ltd
4 Tornay Court, Slapton, Leighton Buzzard LU7 9DA, UK
Tel:    0044 (0) 1525 222 600
Fax:    0044 (0) 1525 222 700
email: boys@neallscott.co.uk
www.aboutourboys.com
www.neallscott.co.uk

Cover design and typesetting by Lesley Fox, Deborah Hawkins and Martin Walker

Printed and distributed by Lulu.com
www.lulu.com

British Library Cataloguing in Publication Data applied for

ISBN 978-1-84753-576-4

*For Peter*

# Contents

# Acknowledgements

I would like to thank the many people who have taken the time to read and comment on what I have written, and whose individual experiences and perspectives have helped shape this book.

Special thanks go to my family, to Lesley Fox and to Shelley Marsh for their long-term support and encouragement. Also to Deborah Hawkins and my editor, Jeremy Mulford, for getting their minds around the detail; and to Jean Hitchen for providing the essential back-up that freed my time and energy.

Lastly, and most importantly, I would like to acknowledge my husband Peter, for his love and support; and my son Conor, who has taught me much and daily shows me the value of this approach.

# Introduction

If you had to sum up what boys are like, what would you say?

Loveable and mischievous? Frustrating and naughty? Interesting and fun? Immature and irritating? Quiet and organised? Noisy and messy? Sport mad? Computer mad? Thirsty for knowledge? So laid back they're horizontal? Straightforward and forgiving? Difficult to understand? Easy to be with? Hard to control?

Your answers will depend on the boys in your life, their ages, their personalities and their temperaments (as well, of course, as your own personality and temperament!).

Boys are individuals who think and behave in individual ways; but despite all the great things our boys get up to individually, boys as a whole aren't getting great press these days. At every stage of school, boys' results are worse than girls'; boys with a spirit of adventure are often thought of as 'trouble'; too often adults who see a group of boys on the street either tell them to move on or fearfully keep their distance; newspapers frequently highlight problems with youths rather than reporting boys' achievements.

Surely this is not what we want for our boys. We want to know that their talents will be made the most of, that their spirit of adventure will be recognised as such, that they are neither seen as a threat nor likely to be threatened.

*What can we as individuals do so that boys thrive, feel happy and motivated, useful and wanted, and become confident, responsible and caring men?*

This book seeks to provide some answers to this question by looking at the nature of boys; what motivates and de-motivates them; how to channel their energy and engage their co-operation; how to give them self-worth and self-discipline; and how to help them deal with their feelings. It does all this in a practical way by offering strategies that can be either used as an overall approach or just tried out from time to time when others' methods don't seem to be working.

The book has had a long gestation period that started when I had a son, now seventeen. I gradually became aware of how different this boy was from me – an adult and a female. A defining moment occurred when I observed an experienced primary school teacher working well with the girls and the quiet and co-operative boys in her class, but responding very unsympathetically to the boisterous boys. Since my son was turning into such a boy and I feared that this teacher's response might not be unusual, I set out to find out what teaching strategies worked best with boys. This led to the publication of my book *Bringing the Best out in Boys – Communication Strategies for Teachers*.

Since then I have spent a lot of time running workshops for teachers, and some schools have asked for a similar session for parents. The turnout for these sessions has often been large, and it quickly became apparent that a second book was needed to adapt my principles and strategies to the home and the community outside school.

Although my first book was aimed at teachers, I also received enquiries from youth clubs and foster-care co-ordinators. The more I thought about it, the more it seemed that this book should explore how boys tick and what adults in any capacity – parents, grandparents, neighbours, aunts, uncles, godparents, youth workers, foster parents, police and probation officers, clergy and local councillors – can do or fail to do, say or not say, to bring out the best in the boys.

It also became clear that it is not enough for an adult to limit their interest in boys to a particular role, such as parent, teacher or youth worker. For what example am I giving if I use my skills to build my own son's self-esteem, but bad-mouth the neighbours' boys; or value the boys that come to the youth club I run, but despise those that prefer to hang out in the street?   Boys who find themselves in a neighbourhood where adults have time for them, treat them respectfully and hold boundaries firm, tend to develop a feeling of responsibility towards that community. Taking a healthy interest in all the boys in the community can make it a better place for your own boys to grow up in.

The aim of this book is to give both men and women an appreciation of where boys are coming from and how they can talk with them, and listen to them, in a way that encourages co-operation and avoids unhelpful conflict. Many adults do this instinctively, creating great rapport with boys at home and in the community. But at times our instinct or experience may not be enough and some extra strategies will be helpful. I hope the suggestions offered are useful at these times. Of course, the way young people respond to an adult depends on where that adult is coming from. They very quickly pick up on the extent of an adult's empathy, firmness and respect – on their true intention. If boys sense that the techniques in the book are being used to manipulate them, then they are unlikely to work.

In attempting to give insights into what boys are like I have, of necessity, made generalisations about the differences between boys and girls, and often refer to boys' 'typical' behaviours. I am aware of the danger and limitations of such generalisations, since both boys and girls present a whole spectrum of temperaments, personalities and behaviours, and many children do not conform to typical male or female norms. In comparing boys and girls there is far more that is the same than is different, so a lot of what you read here may also apply to some or even most girls, and some of what you read won't apply to all the boys you know.

## How to use this book

Each chapter explores a particular topic, first showing how boys may relate to it, then giving practical suggestions to assist in that area. At the end of each chapter there is a summary of key points, followed by some questions or exercises relating to the topic. Many of the points I make are illustrated by stories and examples, and it is worth emphasising that they are all based on actual events and situations.

I would also stress that the approach outlined in this book is not one that comes readily to most of us, and may often run counter to our normal reactions. I therefore suggest you read the book quite quickly to get the philosophy and principles behind it, then go back and practise the skills one chapter at a time. As you are likely to be challenging some deeply engrained habits, give yourself at least a week to apply these new skills before moving on to the next chapter. If possible, discuss the ideas with others and use the questions and exercises at the end of each chapter to explore them further, adapting strategies to individual circumstances and personalities.

A final word before you start: this book explores the nature of boys and how to view them and communicate with them in a way that brings out the best in them. Despite this emphasis, you will find much here that can be applied to any child, adolescent or adult: the principles underlying the ideas and communication skills explored can be used to bring out the best in anyone.

# About Our Boys

# Chapter 1

# Valuing Boys and Giving Them Values

*Treat people as if they were what they ought to be and you help them to become what they are capable of being.*

Goethe

Anyone with youngsters in their lives quickly discovers that boys and girls are different. There are many anecdotes about parents who tried to bring up their sons and daughters without allowing for these differences. Parents whose boys were not allowed toy guns have found them improvising with anything from Lego bricks to crusts of bread. A mother who had filled the playroom with cars and construction kits but no dolls, overheard one daughter saying to the other, 'This one's the mummy car, this one's the daddy car and this one's the baby car.' Parents of twins reported the girl preferring the doll's house while the boy preferred the bow and arrows, neither child being able to persuade their sibling to join them in their chosen game for long.

The way boys often behave is beautifully described by Dan Kindlon and Michael Thompson in their book *Raising Cain:*[1]

*Boys generally are an active lot, and often impulsive. Their energy is contagious, especially among other boys, and that physical energy can translate into a kind of psycho-logical boldness. They often are the risk takers, seemingly oblivious to the potential hurt of a fall or sting of reprimand. Whether their choices might eventually prove to be brave or reckless, boys are often in the middle of an action before they consider the consequences.*

*Boys are direct; they act in simple terms ... Emotional immaturity allows them to celebrate themselves unabashedly, strutting, boasting, clamouring to be noticed. They're not terribly concerned about pleasing others ... Boys' need to feel competent and empowered leads them to express a keen, power-based, action-oriented sense of justice, fairness, good and evil.*

Boys see the world differently from most adults. When trying to understand boys, a good way to start is to consider what it is that they value. It seems to me that most boys value excitement, humour, courage and justice.

---

**Boys value:**
**Excitement✧Humour✧Courage✧Justice**

---

This can apply whether boys are loud or quiet, outgoing or shy, prefer to use their bodies or their minds. Recognising this can give us insights into where boys are coming from and pointers on how to relate well with them.

Most boys seek out excitement, whether in an imaginary game, by speeding about on their bikes, skates or motorbikes, by pushing boundaries to the limit, or by losing themselves in a Playstation adventure.

> *The recipe for fun is pretty simple raising boys: add to any activity an element of danger, stir in a little exploration, add a dash of destruction, and you've got yourself a winner.*
>
> John Eldredge[2]

Humour is an essential element of male life. It is the way males connect with each other, get through bad times, and entertain each other and the opposite sex. How many women have been attracted and entranced by a man's humour, by the outrageousness of it perhaps, but having married him spent the rest of their lives trying to get him to tone his humour down? Boys like to 'have a laugh'; adults can use humour to get boys on side, lighten up a situation and engage co-operation. Boys respect people who can take a joke, and enjoy winding up people who can't.

### *We like messing around, we laugh at everything.*
Christian, aged 12

Boys like to take risks and seem to recognise and value courage in their own and others' actions: a boy who rides his BMX off a high ramp or stands up to someone older than himself is likely to be seen by his peers as brave, even though an adult might think him foolhardy. You will notice boys exercising their 'courage muscle' from an early age. Boys are frequently told not to do things because they are dangerous, but telling a boy something is dangerous may make it more attractive and actually encourage (or en-courage) him to do it!

---

*Why God Made Boys*

*God made a world out of his dreams*
*Of magic mountains, oceans and streams,*
*Prairies and plains and wooded land,*
*Then paused and thought, 'I need someone*
*To stand on top of the mountains, to conquer the sea,*
*Explore the plains and climb the trees,*
*Someone to start out small and grow*
*Sturdy, strong like a tree', and so*
*He created boys, full of spirit and fun*
*To explore and conquer, to romp and run,*
*With dirty faces, banged up chins,*
*With courageous hearts and boyish grins.*
*When he had completed the task he'd begun,*
*He surely said, 'That's a job well done'.*

Cathy Craft, mother of three boys

---

The word courage comes from the French for heart – 'coeur'. One could say that boys express their hearts through their courage.

While all children mind about fairness, boys seem to have an acute sense of justice, reacting strongly to perceived injustices and feeling honour-bound to redress the balance. What boys perceive as unjust, however, may not seem unjust to an adult; nor may their method of redressing the balance seem just to an adult.

Most people, including boys, want and need to be accepted, respected and admired. To what extent do we accept, respect and admire our boys? As a society, I suggest, we are not doing too well, as the following story shows.

*An eleven-year-old boy took a walk by the canal. He soon found some attractive stones to put in his pocket and a long stick to walk with. He seldom came back from a walk without an interesting stone or a good-shaped stick, though sometimes he would settle for a fir cone instead. He spotted some ducks on the path. He crept up to them quietly, seeing how close he could get without frightening them. There was a loud yell from the other side of the canal. The boy started.*

*'Stop harassing the ducks!' a woman shouted from a moored narrow boat. 'Get away from them!'*

*The boy, feeling sullen, for he loved animals and had enjoyed being so close, moved on. The woman watched with hands on hips until she was confident of the ducks' safety. Once the boy had left, a fisherman arrived with his four-year-old daughter. As the man set up his fishing gear, the child played. She spotted the ducks and went towards them, trying to get as close as she could. The woman noted the scene – the fisherman, the little girl and the ducks – and, smiling contentedly, went back into the narrow boat cabin.*

While boys often do get up to mischief, adults must be careful not to assume the worst, not to react to what they think they are seeing rather than what is actually going on.

Such over-reactions leave boys with a deep sense of injustice.

A boy who feels neither accepted nor respected may become resentful, rebellious or disrespectful. If he does not get the admiration he yearns for from adults, he will seek it from his peers, both boys and girls – admiration for his humour, for acting cool or for breaking the rules.

The observation below was made by a male teacher to a group of women, explaining the nature of boys and men.

> *Many women think that men never grow up,*
> *But they've got it wrong:*
> *Men are not large boys,*
> *Boys are little men –*
> *And need to be treated as such.*

A boy who feels valued and respected will show you his best side. Simply making the decision to see the best in the boys in your life will create a positive change in them. Using language to demonstrate that you value them will amplify that change. When boys feel valued by adults, they become interested in taking on the values of those adults.

**To value boys and give them values:**

- Acknowledge a boy's view of the world
- Show admiration for boys' positive qualities
- Give boys respect
- Demonstrate your values in what you do and say

### *Acknowledge a boy's view of the world*

The experience of many boys is that no one really listens to them and that adults are more interested in controlling them than finding out who they are and what they have to say. An effective way to show that you accept and respect someone is to listen to them and acknowledge what they say. Acknowledgment does not imply agreement or approval; it simply demonstrates a desire to understand the other person. If a boy really feels heard and understood, he is likely to give respect and co-operation in return.

Acknowledgment requires only a sincere word or two. Often the less an adult says, the more a boy opens up and draws his own intelligent conclusions. The example below shows how a few words of acknowledgment allowed a seven-year-old boy to sort out a fight without the adult needing to take any action.

Boy: 'Sam hit me!'

Adult: *'I see.'*

Boy: 'I was showing him the karate moves I learnt last week and he suddenly hit me!'

Adult: *'Oh!'*

Boy: 'Maybe he thought I was going to hit him.'

Adult: *'Mmmm.'*

Boy: 'I'll go and tell him I was only showing him how we do it and I'm not going to kick or punch him.

Adult: *'Right.'*

Another simple way of acknowledging a boy's view of the world is to accept and build on what he says:

Whilst doing Maths homework Steven is struggling and wails to his parent, 'It's all gone out of my head!'

*'So it's all gone out of your head, Steven. Let's see if we can get some of it back.'*

It is also important to be able to recognise how boys feel:

Boy:    'I'm bored. There's nothing to do in this stupid place!'

Adult:   *'Life's not much fun when you feel bored.'*

Many women, and some men, find it hard to accept boys' qualities, interests or opinions simply because these are unlike their own childhood experiences, or do not fit with their values. Women often tell me how hard they find it to accept boys' energy and their interest in violence. One father confessed a difficulty in accepting his son's interest in dance; another, who was mad about rugby, could not relate to his son's obsession with football. Even a man dealing with a boy similar to himself as a child can forget what a boy's world is like, sometimes reverting to his own father's habits – replicating his behaviour, using his language and possibly his thoughts. Perhaps the grandfather listened to light opera, and the father to rock and roll, while his son likes hip hop; in each generation the father reacts to his teenage son's music with the same phrase – 'Turn that racket off!'

While an adult may not relate to or agree with a boy's view of the world, it is important that he or she acknowledges that view as real and valid. This allows the boy to experience his own validity. The examples below show

how, when an adult can see the world through the eyes of a boy, it can reap sometimes surprisingly positive responses.

*A woman saw a neighbour's sons on her property, hiding down the side of the garage during a game of 'Manhunt'. She approached them and said: 'Nice hiding place, guys, but it's on my property. Why don't you go and hide over there?' The boys thanked her for the idea and followed her advice.*

*A man walking along the pavement saw three young boys on their BMX bikes; he did not know them. One had been jumping over a milk bottle and left it rolling on the pavement as they rode off.*

*'Excuse me,' the man called. On the second call the boy stopped and turned round. 'I'm seriously impressed by those jumps,' the man said, 'but I don't want anyone walking by to trip over the milk bottle. Can you put it back where you found it?'*

*'I'm sorry!' responded the boy and returned the milk bottle to the doorstep.*

*Some teenage boys were hanging around at the end of an alley; one was sitting on the pavement. A woman walking down the alley saw them at the end. It was difficult to ignore them, so she decided to engage with them instead. 'You look like you're having a good time,' she said The boy sitting on the pavement looked up at her. 'We like you,' he said.*

In these examples the adult sees the world through the eyes of the boys – they are having some fun. Although from the boys' point of view what they are doing is harmless, from an adult's point of view the teenagers in the alley may appear threatening, the youngsters playing manhunt are trespassing, and the boys on their bikes could seem like vandals. It is not uncommon these days for groups of boys to be seen in this way, and sometimes it is true. But such perceptions risk becoming self-fulfilling. If boys are feared and no one engages with them, they become isolated and operate by their own rules. If boys are confronted without some understanding, they feel aggrieved and may be rude or refuse to co-operate. Recognising their view of the world makes it easier for them to co-operate.

Acknowledgment can take you a long way, even – or especially – when boys seem to be behaving unreasonably.

*A music festival has been organised in the park and as a result the skateboarding area is out of use for the day; a notice about it has been up for weeks. Whilst most young people are pleased to have a festival, the skateboarders and BMX riders are unhappy. They gather outside the skate park, complaining that their facility has been taken away.*

Instead of: 'I don't know what you're complaining about. It's only one day out of 365, and you had loads of notice. You should consider yourselves lucky to live in a town that has a skate park and a music festival.'

say: *'I can see you're really annoyed that you can't use the skate park for a whole day. I don't*

*think anyone realised how much you'd all
mind. When we organise next year's festival it
would be really good if you came along to say
what you think and helped us come up with a
better way of doing it.'*

It is easy to misinterpret boys' natural curiosity and sense of
mischief or adventure as bad behaviour – for example,
when they take something apart, make a 'potion' out of
every liquid in the kitchen, play a practical joke or build a
fire. Many adults see these things as destructive, dangerous
or anti-social, but the only real problem is the time and the
place.

Instead of:  'You've completely destroyed that. You break
everything!'

say:  *'It looks like you wanted to see how that works.
It'll be harder putting it back together again –
do you want some help?'*

Instead of:  'What on earth are you up to? Look at the state
of the kitchen! How dare you use all these
things without asking!'

say:  *'Whoa! Seems like there's a major experiment
going on in here! Now we need a few ground
rules: you can use anything from this
cupboard, nothing from that cupboard and I'll
see what you can use from the fridge. On one
condition though – the kitchen's left spotless
when you're done. Will you agree to that?
There'll be an inspection!'*

Instead of: 'Mr Jones told me he caught you and your friends lighting a fire on the waste ground. You know fires are dangerous. Why did you do such a stupid thing?'

say: *'Mr Jones told me he caught you and your friends lighting a fire on the waste ground. I know fires are fascinating, but you are not to light them up there. Let's make a fire pit in the garden, then you'll be able to have a fire without upsetting other people.'*

Instead of: 'There is nothing funny about 'knock and run'! You were victimising that old lady. Next time you do anything like that you'll be reported to the police!'

say: *'I can see that it might seem funny, her coming to the door and no one being there. However, look at it from her point of view. She's got arthritis and even walking to the front door is painful. No wonder she gets angry when there's no one there! I'd like you to apologise to her. Are you up to going on your own or would you rather I came with you?'*

One way to get an angle on where boys are coming from is to ask them.

To a boy who declares he hates school:
*'Sounds like you've had a bad day. How did it go?*

To a boy who listens to lyrics that don't appeal to you:

*'I'm not sure about those lyrics. What are they trying to say?'*

Then after he's explained:

*'And what do you think?'*

Listening to boys' views can help you see a situation in a different light:

*The five-a-side football club has become a victim of its own success and lots of boys turn up for a game. They have loads of energy to burn off: away from the pitch this converts to noise and jostling, with bigger boys chasing and pinning down smaller ones; on the pitch it becomes rough play and little consideration for others. The coach has to referee very tightly to keep a lid on the game and can no longer trust those waiting their turn to behave. All his energy and attention are used to keep control, and he realises he no longer enjoys running the club.*

*He decides to ask the opinions of some of the boys involved. The older ones say that they would like to play for longer and don't like all the waiting around. The younger ones say the older ones are too rough and recommend splitting the club by age, maybe playing on different days. The coach mulls this over: yesterday he was considering closing the club and, to his surprise, today he is considering doing two sessions a week.*

*In the event, he changes from one hour-and-a-half session to two one-hour sessions for different age groups. The boys are calmer and more responsible, the coach is able to concentrate on improving skill levels rather than crowd control, and he finds his previous enthusiasm for the club has returned.*

There are situations when an adult getting into a discussion with boys about why or how things should be done would be unhelpful – they simply need to be done. In some instances, however, potentially confrontational situations can be avoided by asking a boy to explain his point of view, as shown in these examples:

*A boy often gets angry when he is punished and you suspect he has felt unfairly treated in the past.*

After you give him a sanction you might say:

*'Do you think I dealt with that fairly?'*

A boy who repeatedly breaks a rule might be asked:

*'Is there anything about this rule you don't understand or don't agree with?'*

This will only work if your voice demonstrates you are genuinely interested in his point of view; if there is any hint of sarcasm, the approach will backfire.

It is important to listen to his reply and acknowledge his point of view, even if you don't agree with it.

*Since Jess has heard he has not been picked for team, he is snappy with everyone.*

Instead of:          'Just because you aren't in the team you don't have to take it out on everyone else!'

say (privately):     *'Are you upset not to be in the team?'*

*A boy is showing little interest in the homework project he has been asked to do. When the parent tries to encourage him to get on with it, the boy says it's boring.*

Instead of: 'It's only boring because you're making it boring.'

ask: *'What makes it boring – too hard / too easy / too much writing / you aren't interested in the subject?'*

(If you ask a boy why something is boring without giving him some options, he may not be able to give you a useful reply.)

Acknowledging someone's reality can be difficult when you think it is wrong, but it can save a lot of disagreement.

*Six-year-old Jason comes onto the sofa, pushing his younger sister Jane from where she was sitting. Jane objects loudly and tells their father. Jason insists it is his place. As far as their father is concerned there is no such thing as 'my place' (even though one of the armchairs is known as 'Dad's chair').*

Instead of: 'Don't be ridiculous Jason, Jane was not sitting in your place.'
('Oh yes she was!')

say: *'So Jane was sitting where you wanted to sit, Jason. If you want something, you ask. You do not push or hurt.'*

By moving in the boy's direction you make it easier for him to come towards you in response.

The same applies when boys choose to explore the 'dark side'. Whilst many boys, especially when they are young, identify with heroes, as they get older some want to explore what it is to be the anti-hero. To be the good guy can seem a bit tame and conventional, while the bad guy is more exciting and allows the boy to explore the wild male within.[3] This can seem unappealing and worrying to the adults around him, and may be hard to accept. Adults who find little difficulty in embracing a boy's roles of Batman, Spiderman, Robin Hood, Luke Skywalker, Aragorn or a sports idol may find it less palatable when the boy plays the roles of the Green Goblin, Darth Vader, an ork or a vampire (particularly when this involves pretty gruesome play-acting), or later identifies with anti-establishment teenage groups.

My feeling is that it is actually healthy to allow boys to work through these areas in the relative safety of childhood, so that they can grow out of them and move on; the experiences will help them develop a moral code for adulthood. If adults allow boys to explore these roles openly, they are in a position to discuss the ideas with them and place boundaries on their behaviour. Disapproval, ridicule or prohibition may force boys into clandestine play. Alternatively, the boy may push these thoughts, unexplored, into the recesses of his mind, from where they may emerge in his adult life as, for example, explosive anger or depression. So don't get unduly worried when boys explore the 'dark side'; but do keep your eyes and ears open, stay involved and keep communication channels open.

### *Show admiration for boys' positive qualities*

Boys seek admiration from many places, but I suspect that most boys would want to be admired first and foremost by their father. The father is the person from whom a boy can learn what it is to be a man: if he gets the admiration of his father, if he experiences his dad being proud of him, then he feels he is being accepted into the tribe of men.

Some boys do not receive the admiration of their father: perhaps because the father is not there; perhaps because he is not very involved with the family; perhaps because he is so keen for his son to do well that he only points out the boy's shortcomings; perhaps because his own father did not show him admiration. It was at his father's funeral that my husband discovered how proud his father had been of him: one of his father's former work colleagues told him how much his father had spoken about him at work. He had longed for this acknowledgement as a boy and as a man, but his father was not someone who talked to his children in this way.

If a boy does not get admiration from his father, he will look to other adult men for it – to his step-father or foster father, his uncle, grown-up brother, grandfather, youth worker, teacher or neighbour. He wants to be recognised as a 'young man' and will choose his role models from those who recognise him as such.

With the increase in divorce rates, single-parent families and step-families, it is important for boys to have a father figure or positive male role model who can share in their lives. The Topman *Leading Lads* survey[4] analysed the

23

views and experiences of 1,344 teenage boys and found that the level of involvement of a father or father figure had a significant effect on boys' self-esteem and was more important than whether or not he lived with the boy:

*This study suggests that whether a father is resident or non-resident may impact less than the quality of his fathering. Some fathers are present in the home but not emotionally available to their sons. Excessive work hours and stress contribute to fathers being described as 'there, but not for me', or 'the stranger who comes to Sunday lunch'.*

If a boy does not find acceptance and approval from men, then he will look to older boys or peers in order to belong. This is where gang culture becomes dangerous, with values being learnt from young males who know nothing about manhood. A boy who has strong, positive, adult male role models may flirt with a gang or teenage group, but he is likely to come out of it relatively unscathed; a boy without positive adult role models is much more vulnerable to peer pressure.

A boy also wants to be admired by the females in his life. This is different from love or praise; it is a validation by a woman of the boy's maleness, and will give him confidence in his masculinity. And if women do not recognise his wit, dress-sense, courage, ability at sport, or his sensitivity and ability to listen, then no doubt some girls will. Have you noticed how even the 'nicest' girls can be enthralled by boys' outrageous stories or 'off-the-wall' behaviour?

Adults can validate boys and their maleness by finding things about them to admire.

*'Nice haircut, Tim.'*
*'Come on Jack, show us how it's done!'*
*'You do make me laugh!'*
*'You certainly know your way round a computer.'*
*'That was brave.'*
*'How on earth do you do that?'*
*'Good man!'*

Adults can also demonstrate admiration for qualities that boys have not yet learned to value.

*'You've been practising on your new roller blades all week. You're really getting the hang of it.'*

*'Thank you for looking after your sister on her first day at your school.'*

*'You got down to your homework, then went out with your friends. It's great to see you taking charge of your life.'*

*'You being honest about breaking that window means we can sort it out without me getting angry.'*

Birthday cards are a great opportunity to acknowledge what you admire in a boy. So are 'un-birthday cards', which can be written at any time during the year. An unexpected card in the post can contain a message that can be read and treasured privately. Parents can leave occasional notes acknowledging their son on his pillow – after a difficult time a positive note can move things on.

*HAPPY BIRTHDAY*
*to someone with*
*a great imagination and*
*a wonderful smile*

*Let's find a time to do something*
*together when I'm home.*
*I am proud of the young man*
*you are growing into.*
*LOVE DAD*

*I really appreciated*
*you mending the*
*computer today –*
*THANK YOU!*

*HAPPY BIRTHDAY*
*Thanks for looking after*
*me every day.*
*With love from your hamster*
*Trevor*

### Give boys respect

Suppose a group of boys are playing football in your neighbourhood. They may be seven or eight years old, they may be fourteen or fifteen. A woman comes out of her house and sees them. Do you think she would say something like: 'Hi boys. You seem to be having a good game there – nice shot Michael. I'm a bit worried about the ball hitting the cars. Would you go and play down the park?'

When working with teachers, I often describe this scenario and ask what response their boys might get. In the many schools I've worked with, the answer is almost always the same: she would tell the boys to go away, probably in a loud disrespectful voice and possibly using obscene language. No courtesy, no empathy. If this is the way boys experience being treated by adults in their neighbourhood, is it any wonder they don't always treat adults respectfully?

Some people believe that respect should be earned, and only give it to those they deem worthy of it. I imagine many boys would agree with this view. Unfortunately it usually results in a stalemate: an adult won't show respect to a boy because he is not respectful or respect-worthy; a boy won't show respect to an adult because he or she does not seem respectful or respect-worthy. If we want boys to be respectful, the best way to teach them is by example.

When boys do feel respected, they respond incredibly well:

27

**About Our Boys**

*A man in the cinema turned round to tell some boys to be quiet. When he passed their row at the end of the film, he thanked them. The boys' mouths dropped open in surprise: rebukes they were used to, gratitude they weren't.*

*A youth worker told two boys off for something he thought they had done. Agitated, the boys protested that they hadn't done it. The youth worker realised he had been wrong, so apologised for the mistake. Their protests stopped immediately, but the respect the youth worker got from that incident lasted for years.*

*A woman was returning to her car in a multi-storey car park when she came across three boys skateboarding. 'Do you know there's CCTV in here?' she asked them.*

*'It doesn't work,' they assured her.*

*The oldest boy jumped up and pulled at a metal sign on one of the pillars.*

*'Personally I've no problem with you skateboarding in here,' the woman said, 'but I don't like you damaging the car park.'*

*The older boy carried on, but one of the younger boys appealed to him: 'She asked you nicely, Tom.' Unwillingly, the older boy stopped.*

*'Thanks,' said the woman. 'Enjoy your skateboarding'. And she went to find her car.*

Boys hate being backed into a corner, and often react by fighting back, even when they know it's a lost cause.

> *Males are like juggernauts – they can carry a big load but they need a large turning circle.*
>
> Bob Pearce, father of two boys

Challenging boys in a confrontational way frequently provokes challenging behaviour; a non-confrontational approach is likely to get a more positive response. Be sensitive to male pride and allow boys an honourable way out.

Instead of:     humiliating them in front of other people

whisper:     *'I saw that.'*

Instead of:     insisting on a particular course of action

offer choices:     *'Do you want to repair the damage or pay for someone else to?'*

Instead of:     being controlling or heavy about an issue

use humour:     *'The next person who comes in the house with muddy shoes will be put head first into the compost bin!'*

Being respectful to boys does not equate to tolerating disrespect from them, but it does mean addressing disrespectful behaviour in a respectful way:

Instead of:   'How dare you use that language in front of my
              children!'

say:          *'My kids are a bit young to hear that kind of
              language. And to tell you the truth, I don't like
              it either. I'd appreciate it if you didn't swear
              when we can hear you. Would you do that for
              me?'*

Notice that the question to the boy in the last example
started with 'would you' rather than 'could you'. In *Men are
from Mars and Women are from Venus*, John Gray observes
that men often interpret 'could you' literally – as 'are you
able' rather than 'will you'. The same applies to boys; so
when you ask them to do something, 'would' is often more
effective than 'could'.

When all is said and done, respect is really about assuming
the best in people and treating them as you would like to be
treated.

*A middle-aged couple arrived at an unmanned railway
station. On the platform were a dozen teenage boys
carrying plastic bags that looked as though they contained
cans of beer. The couple would have to pass the group to
cross the footbridge to their platform. Being familiar with
the station, the woman knew that the boys must be on the
wrong platform.*

*'Excuse me,' she said. 'No trains stop on this platform.
Where are you going?'*

*One of the boys told her their destination. She directed him
to the correct platform.*

*'You are the best!' he told her.*

*The couple found themselves on the opposite platform to the group of boys, who were horsing around and teasing one another. One of the boys was Asian, and his friends were ribbing him, saying that there weren't trains in India. The man called over to them, 'India has one of the best railway networks in the world!'*

*The boy looked grateful.*

*Another boy shouted across to the couple, 'Where are you going?*

*'To London,' replied the woman. 'My husband is seeing me off.'*

*The boy saw the train approaching in the distance and shouted to the man, 'Her train is coming – you had better kiss her goodbye!'*

*The couple embraced to the sounds of cheering and clapping from the other platform, and the man put his wife safely on the train.*

### Demonstrate your values in what you do and say

Boys will pick up values from the adults around them, particularly those they love or admire. Different people have different values, and a commentary on what you are doing or what you expect of others can help make it clear to boys what your values are.

You want boys to respect their environment and not to leave litter:

*'Let's put our litter in the bin and leave this place just as we found it.'*

*'Look at that litter someone's left behind. It looks horrible. Let's clean it up.'*

*'Someone told me about a sign they saw in a national park in Canada. It said, "Leave only footprints, take only photographs".'*

You want boys to be kind to others:

*'That boy looks a bit lonely. Let's go over and talk to him.'*

*'Thanks for helping me in with the shopping.'*

*'Isn't it great that people help each other out in this neighbourhood.'*

Values will be conveyed through the way we talk about our lives, our work and other people, through the opinions we express and the anecdotes we tell. Boys learn as much from what we do as from what we say. If they see their parents being affectionate, they'll learn about love; if they hear adults speaking respectfully to each other, they'll understand respect; if they are around people who are polite to one another, then courtesy will come more naturally to them.

---

**Values are caught not taught**

---

Men can teach boys to respect women through their own actions and words. Women play an important role in teaching boys (and their sisters) respect for men. If children hear their mother talking about their father and other men with affection and respect, they will take on these values. If their mother puts their father down, children may learn to despise men in general and their father in particular. This causes obvious difficulties for a boy, since he will grow up to be a man himself.

It is worth considering to what extent we live the values we espouse. If what we say and what we do are inconsistent, then boys get mixed messages.

*When Paul was six years old, he was with his father when he dumped building rubble at the side of the road to avoid paying for it at the tip.*
*'It's OK son,' his father said as they drove off, 'everyone does it.'*

*When Paul was eight, he sat in on a family meeting discussing how to reduce the tax on the family business.*
*'It's OK kid, everybody does it,' said his uncle.*

*When he was eleven, his aunt took him and his older sister out to a Chinese restaurant that offered free meals for under-elevens. His aunt told the waiter the children were under 11.*
*'It's OK, everybody does it,' she said.*

*When he was twelve, he broke his glasses on the way to school. His mum convinced the insurance company they had been stolen and got £50 back.*
*'It's OK,' she said, 'everybody does it.'*

*When he was fifteen, he made the rugby team, and the
coach showed him how to hurt the other players without the
referee seeing.*
*'It's OK,' he said, 'everybody does it.'*

*When he was sixteen, he worked at the market and was
shown how to put over-ripe tomatoes beneath the ripe ones
in the shoppers' bags.*
*'It's OK,' said the stallholder, 'everyone does it.'*

*At university he was not a great student, so when he was
offered the exam questions for £10 because everybody did
it, he took them.*

*He was caught, and sent home in disgrace.*

*'How could you do this to us?' said his dad. 'You never
learned anything like that from home!'[5]*

Honour may seem an old-fashioned concept, but it is one to
which boys relate strongly, even if they are not familiar
with the word. Honour underlies the stories of good versus
evil that many boys respond well to, such as King Arthur,
Robin Hood, Harry Potter, Star Wars, Lord of the Rings,
Greek mythology and The Chronicles of Narnia. Left to
their own devices, boys will create their own 'honour code',
which may include things like not telling on your friends
and getting your own back on people who treat you badly.

The concept of honour can be used to explore values with
boys. Andy Loveless coaches an under-ten boys' football
team. He discussed the behaviours of winners and losers
with the boys, who then came up with a code of conduct for
their team.

## Team Code of Conduct

### Winners

1. Arrive early for training and matches
2. Listen to coaches and team-mates
3. Tackle fairly and safely in training
4. Lose honourably
5. Win honourably
6. Shake hands at the end of a match
7. Ask questions during training sessions
8. Have a good night's sleep before the match

### Losers

1. Arrive at the last minute or are late
2. Backchat and don't listen
3. Tackle badly and kick team-mates
4. Sulk or get angry when they lose
5. Gloat or crow when they win
6. Ignore their opponents at the end of the match
7. Think they know best during training sessions
8. Turn up tired and emotional to training sessions and matches

CHAPTER SUMMARY

# Valuing Boys and Giving Them Values

### Acknowledge a boy's view of the world
- Try to see the world through the eyes of a boy
- Recognise boys' need for excitement, humour, courage and justice
- Empathise with boys' thoughts and feelings
- Acknowledge their point of view, even when you don't agree with it

### Show admiration for boys' positive qualities
- Find admirable qualities in boys
- Tell them what you admire
- Show admiration for qualities they haven't yet learned to value

### Give boys respect
- Teach respect by your example
- Treat boys as people, not problems
- Give boys an honourable way out

### Demonstrate your values in what you do and say
- Most values are caught, not taught
- Explaining values can make them clearer
- As boys get older, discuss values with them

NOTEBOOK

Is there anything about boys you find particularly difficult to relate to? (You may want to answer this first with regard to boys in general, and then try to answer it with regard to particular boys.)

What might you do or say (or not do/say) to show empathy for where a boy is coming from?

Think of a few things you admire about particular boys. What could you do or say to show your admiration?

Think of circumstances where boys may feel disrespected by adults.

In such instances, what exactly would boys interpret as disrespectful?

How could the adult have behaved differently?

What values do you think it is important for boys to have?

How do/can you demonstrate those values when you are with boys?

How might you discuss these values with boys without it becoming a lecture?

**Exploring Tone of Voice and Body Language**

Tone of voice and body language can determine the way a message is received, so it is worth being aware of our own communication style. The following exercise enables you to explore how you might come across in particular situations.

Try saying the sentences below to someone else at different volumes and in different tones of voice. Ask them to imagine they are a boy and to tell you how they might respond. Do you sound firm and respectful? Does your tone of voice, facial expression or body language convey any additional, particularly negative, messages?

- I said No.
- Stop what you are doing and come here, please.
- It's bedtime.
- Where are you going?
- Do not hit other children.
- I don't want to have to tell you again.
- Be quiet.
- You can watch TV when you've done your homework.
- I heard that.
- I'm very angry.

Make a note of any situations where your tone of voice or body language might seem disrespectful, and think of ways you can adjust them to make sure you convey respect.

## Chapter 2

# Channelling Boys' Energy

*Huck Finn is drawn from life; Tom Sawyer also ... he is the composition of three boys I knew. ... Part of my plan has been to pleasantly remind adults of what they once were themselves, and of how they felt and thought and talked, and what queer enterprises they sometimes engaged in.*

Mark Twain, 1876

Boys are typically energetic, action-orientated and physical. Even those boys who don't like sport or aren't very active usually have active minds that are drawn to action and adventure in their imaginary play, computer games, the books they like and the films they watch.

It is essential that boys be allowed to be physical and do activities that use up their energy. This is becoming harder than it used to be. In previous generations many children were allowed to 'play out' for long periods, having unsupervised games and adventures. Most people in the community knew the children, so misdemeanours were dealt with directly, or parents were told what their children were up to. In this age of busy roads, concerns about safety, dispersed communities and a culture of blame, parents are less happy to allow children to be out and children are less welcome on the street.

I once watched a group of boys, aged between six and fourteen, climbing a tree in the village where I live; they were having a great time. A father of one of the younger boys arrived, told his son to come down because it was dangerous, and made it clear to the others he thought they were doing wrong.

'Didn't you climb trees when you were a boy?' I asked him.

'Yes,' he replied, 'but only in my own garden.'

Unfortunately most boys are not lucky enough to have a climbing tree in their own garden, and have always had to go further a field to get this basic childhood experience.

When boys are told off for the relatively harmless activity of climbing a tree, what will they choose to do instead? Maybe they'll go to the park and play football and use up their energy that way. Perhaps they'll just 'hang out' and chat; but how long will it be before they'll feel the need to do something physical or exciting? If they are still in an adventurous mood, will they decide to throw stones or light a fire; or will smoking or drugs satisfy their taste for adventure? Perhaps they will go home and sit in front of a DVD or a playstation. Maybe they'll choose an exciting film or game, possibly a violent one, and instead of dissipating their energy physically through exercise, their adrenalin will build up and burst out later in the day.

The modern trend of overprotecting children from physical dangers brings with it other, possibly greater, dangers. Boys who are not allowed to do what comes naturally to them, or who are tightly chaperoned, will not develop important abilities and attributes such as responsibility, assessing risk, looking after themselves, judgment, independence and time-keeping.

---

**Free Running**

Boys are finding ways of expressing their adventurous spirit in the modern town and city. Skateboarders use shopping centres, car parks and underpasses to practise their skills. In-line skaters stretch their abilities by using curbs and railings to develop new rollerblade techniques. Young men have invented a sport called 'free running' or 'parkour'. They devise an obstacle course using walls, roofs and fences and run the course performing a series of jumps, vaults and tumbles, thereby transforming the urban landscape into an adventure playground.

---

## The biology of boys

Research into gender shows that there are significant physiological and behavioural differences between boys and girls.[1]

- In the first few hours of life, baby girls are much more interested in people and faces, while baby boys are as happy if objects are dangled in front of them.
- On average, girls say their first words and learn to speak in short sentences earlier than boys.
- Boys are generally more active than girls, moving faster and spending more time in motion.[2]

–     Girls tend to read earlier than boys and find it easier to cope with grammar, spelling and punctuation.
–     Boys tend to have better spatial ability, which gives them superior hand/foot-eye co-ordination and enables them to visualise easily in three-dimensions.
–     Girls spend more time talking and listening than most boys.

Hearing and sight also differ between boys and girls:

–     Girls are more sensitive to noise than most boys, have wider peripheral vision and can see better in the dark.
–     Boys tend to see better in bright light, have a greater sense of perspective and observe in a more focused way.
–     Girls are generally better at understanding verbal and visual nuances in communication.
–     Young boys tend to have growth spurts that affect their ear canals: the ear canal stretches, thins and often blocks up, leading to periods of hearing loss.[3]

Differences have been found between male and female brains. The typical male brain is much more specialised than the female brain, with functions such as vocabulary, visuo-spacial perception and emotion being located only in one or other side of the brain. In a typical female brain, these functions are located in both sides and the bundle of connections that joins the two hemispheres is thicker than in the male brain.

And what about testosterone, the hormone often blamed for the behaviour of adolescent boys? Testosterone starts to be made in the male embryo around the sixth week of pregnancy. This stimulates the development of the male sexual organs, lays down the blueprint for the neural pathways, and programmes the brain to respond to increases in testosterone levels later in life. Once the testicles are formed, they produce additional testosterone, and by the time the baby is born he has as much testosterone flowing around his body as a twelve-year-old boy. A few months after birth the testosterone level in boys falls away. The level then remains similar to that of girls throughout babyhood and toddlerhood.

Boys experience their next surge of testosterone at the age of four and tend to become more interested in action, adventure and vigorous play. At five, testosterone levels drop again, and the hormone levels in boys and girls are roughly equivalent for a few years. Boys' testosterone levels rise sharply between eleven and thirteen, causing sudden growth that requires some 'rewiring' of the nervous system to keep pace with these changes. As a result of the building programme taking place in his body, a boy can become temporarily clumsy, disorganised and dopey during these years.[4]

Testosterone levels reach their peak in boys at around fourteen. This increases body muscle, prompts the voice to break and generates strong sexual feelings, general restlessness and a desire to test limits. It also affects the way the brain functions: IQ tests show that between the ages of fourteen and sixteen boys catch up with girls in writing and verbal ability and surge ahead in mathematical ability (whether this ability is realised will depend on a variety of other factors, especially their relationship with school).

Research, into both humans and animals, shows that testosterone produces energetic and boisterous behaviour, risk-taking and single-mindedness, self-confidence and self-reliance, competitiveness and a need for hierarchy.

## Energy management

If the energetic nature of boys is managed and channelled appropriately, they will thrive. If their energy is seen as disruptive, something to be suppressed and controlled, then boys will feel misunderstood and may become disaffected, confrontational, withdrawn or compliant.

What's wrong with a compliant boy, you might ask: don't we want boys to be obedient and respectful? We do, but we also want them to have a strong sense of self, from which stems self-discipline, self-esteem and self-confidence. If boys are treated in a controlling way, their sense of self can be crushed; they become obedient, but their spirit may die. The following story illustrates how this can happen.

*There was once a girl who found school difficult and unpleasant; her name was Kathy. She was dyslexic at a time before dyslexia was commonly recognised, and was teased throughout her school career. As a teenager she was befriended by a boy who protected and cared for her. Eventually they got married. In reaction to her childhood, Kathy decided on a survival strategy for adulthood – to be in control. She took charge of the house and the family, had strong views about what should and should not be done, and made sure her rules were abided by. The more Kathy took charge, the more her husband deferred to her. At first it pleased her to have her way, but she soon became irritated by his apparent weakness, and critical of many of the things he did. The couple's first son had the temperament of his father and Kathy found him easy to control. Their second son was more spirited. When the children were small, Kathy was heard expressing pride in her youngest – who was brave and adventurous and stuck up for himself – comparing him favourably to the older one. But as the youngest grew he started to want his own way, to have his own opinions, to come into the house messy, to break the rules. This would not do. The pride Kathy had felt when he was younger became irritation: his behaviour did not fit into Kathy's worldview: her youngest had to be tamed. Kathy set out to control her family. She was successful, but the cost was high – in the process she lost her admiration for her husband and her sons, and they lost touch with their masculinity.*

### To channel boys' energy:

- Give boys opportunities to express their physical energy
- Keep boys stimulated and challenged
- Use humour to get boys on side
- Set boys up to succeed

### *Give boys opportunities to express their physical energy*

Boys need opportunities to burn off their physical energy. This keeps them occupied, leaves them calmer, and is good for health, fitness and sleep. After a growth spurt a boy can become clumsy in his larger body, being not yet fully aware of where it ends. Physical activity aids co-ordination as he gets used to his new shape and size.

Boys need time and space to be physical, indoors as well as outside. When they are young, activities do not need to be particularly structured and most boys like doing things that have a sense of adventure: jumping on a mattress or a trampoline; building a den; play fighting; climbing trees; exploring; going out in the rain; playing in the mud; having a camp fire in the garden; transforming a room into another world.

As boys get older they may need more organised activities. A boy who likes sports has an obvious outlet for his physical energy.

> *I'm glad my son has taken up cricket: it takes up so much of his time that he's unlikely to get bored and get into trouble.*
>
> Mother of boy aged 12

Used well, sport not only channels a boy's energy but can teach him about teamwork, commitment, discipline and the value of practice – lessons that can be transferred to other parts of his life. If the purpose of the sport is to channel a boy's energy, then adults should be wary of getting too attached to his performance. A teacher told me of the negative effects she regularly saw when parents came to support their sons at school matches. At the end of the match, instead of congratulating the boy on the times he had played well, or commiserating with him on what had gone badly, parents would tell their sons when and how they should have played better. This gives the boy the message that to be loved he has to win. Such childhood experiences have caused many a man to go through life constantly trying to prove himself.

Boys who don't enjoy team games may prefer other activities, e.g. martial arts, skating, gym, archery, cycling, swimming, dancing, playing music, fishing, dog walking or playing with a frisbee. Older boys can benefit from outdoor pursuits, which may reveal qualities less apparent at home.

## Fighting, weapons and violence

Parents are often concerned about boys' attraction to violence, and worry that allowing them to fight and to play with weapons will encourage aggressiveness. I have come to the conclusion that boys need to explore and understand their aggression while they are too small to do much damage and young enough to accept parental guidance.

Play fighting is an essential part of a boy's childhood. Boys love to fight with adults and it provides a wonderful way to be physically intimate, to gain confidence, to teach self-control (stick to the rules), and to show who is boss. I remember a visit from my brother when my stepson was eight. He and a friend were thrilled to have an adult playmate, and spent the evening wrestling with him. To their astonishment, two against one gave them no advantage, and whatever moves they tried resulted in them both being pinned down. Years later I witnessed a similar scene. This time my stepson was the adult and the boys were my son and a friend. The boys thought they were invincible, but found themselves thwarted at every turn and, mystified, finally admitted defeat.

One of the games we played with our son was the 'bed fight', where the double bed became a wrestling ring. The adult would make sure the child didn't fall off when he was small; but when he was bigger, falling off was all part of the fun. This developed into a Saturday morning ritual, and since my husband was much more exciting to fight with than me, I was sent to soak in the bath with a book while they tussled.

Wrestling is a useful way for boys to learn and practise self-defence. Whether or not a boy actually needs this skill later in life, knowing he can defend himself will give him self-confidence, which may keep him out of trouble or prevent him from being bullied. My husband was brought up in a family that did not allow fighting or toy weapons – any child who fought was hit with the back of a hairbrush! He reports having felt scared or incapable when faced with someone that was prepared to use force. In his thirties he admitted this to a friend who had been brought up in a tough part of London. The friend gave him some self-defence lessons, and despite never having had to use them, he now feels he could protect himself or his family if the need arose.

Many boys benefit from the discipline of martial arts, such as tae kwondo, karate or boxing. These can calm aggressive boys and give confidence to quieter boys. Where fighting is permitted, boundaries need to be made clear to boys (more about boundaries in Chapter 3). If the rules are broken, the fight is stopped.

*The youth club was for eight- to sixteen-year-olds and there were far more boys in the neighbourhood than girls. Despite a clear 'no fighting' policy, every week the youth workers would have to break up two or three 'play fights' amongst the boys. One week they tried a different tack: they laid out some mats in the corner of the hall and told the boys that if they wanted to fight they had to do it on the mats – anyone on the mats could fight, anyone off the mats could not. This was the birth of the 'bundle corner', which was popular and effective in channelling the boys' energy.*

*The boys agreed on some rules (shoes off and certain moves not permitted). The first week, it was a male domain, but soon both girls and boys enjoyed it, setting up their own timetable (little ones/ middle-sized ones/ big ones, boys/girls/mixed). Sometimes they asked permission for a mixed-age group 'bundle' and the ten-year-old boys were thrilled to be picked up and dropped on cushions by sixteen-year-old lads.*

*As the months went on and that particular group of children grew older, the bundle corner was requested less often and other activities became more popular.*

This 'bundle corner' was invented in response to a particular situation, and it worked with a particular group of children.

Another set of boys might have got out of hand; in which case the idea would have been adapted or abandoned. As an adult you can only respond to the situation presented, and use your instincts to determine what might work. You won't always get it right, but if one approach doesn't work, you can always try something else.

If play fighting may actually be healthy, what about weapons? A few generations ago it was considered normal for boys to play with guns, swords, bows and arrows. Now there is much debate as to whether letting boys play with weapons encourages violence. I think toy weapons are acceptable as long as they are not used to hurt or frighten, so may require rules like 'only use them in the house/garden'. I once witnessed a father on a family camp berating other parents for allowing their children to bring toy guns. I have seldom seen such pent-up aggression in a person: the father was preaching non-violence, but his whole body conveyed the opposite. It struck me that the boys who had brought the guns to camp were likely to grow up having a healthier relationship with aggression than the sons of this angry man who forbade toy weapons.

The other concern is violence on TV and in computer games. It is relatively easy to control young children's viewing and access to games and computers in the home, except when they want to join in with the games and viewing of older brothers and sisters. As boys get older, however, many will be drawn towards gory and aggressive adventures that their mothers, in particular, may find unpalatable. For many boys, violent films or games provide a means of temporary escape into a simple and enjoyable world of fighting and action. The question may not be whether boys should have any access to violent viewing, but about what, when, where, with whom, for how long and at what age. Instead of having TVs and computers in the bedroom where they can be used unsupervised, put them in a family space where use is negotiated, limited and supervised. Watch out for mood swings and behaviour changes after viewing, and explain to boys that negative behaviour will result in reduced viewing. Each family will make their own decisions; if you permit a certain amount of 'violent' viewing and play at home, it literally allows you to keep an eye on it.

*A nine-year-old boy came back from a sleepover with a friend, raving about the WWF (World Wrestling Federation) fights he had watched on television. The mother was horrified: she had never seen WWF, but from everything her son said it sounded violent and offensive.*

*She became concerned over the next few days as he talked obsessively about it and practised apparently dangerous moves on other boys. When she told them of her distaste for it, her son reassured her: 'Don't worry, Mum, it's not really violent: the wrestlers practise before the show – all the moves are choreographed.'*

*She wasn't convinced: 'But those moves you talk about sound pretty vicious – surely the wrestlers get hurt sometimes?'*

*Yes, the boy conceded, the wrestlers did get injured sometimes, but mostly it was a carefully choreographed performance to entertain the audience.*

*The mother left it at that and was relieved when, after seeing the* Star Wars *'Phantom Menace' movie, the boys seemed to have moved on from WWF. The film's heroes had fought with double-ended light-sabres, and the boys used sticks to simulate them.*

*One day she looked out into the garden to see two boys fighting with sticks and heard her son saying, 'No, no, you've done it wrong – you're supposed to take two steps back now.'*

*The boys had choreographed their fight – perhaps something positive had been taken from WWF after all.*

### Keep boys stimulated and challenged

Energy is not just in boys' bodies; it is also in their minds. Their need for adventure and excitement can be met in their imagination and in the games that they play. Contrary to the common perception that boys have short attention spans, they have great concentration when, for example, model building, watching a thriller, playing a computer game or finding out about their favourite subject.

During a radio interview, a master of the choir school at King's College, Cambridge, was asked how they prevented choristers misbehaving. His reply was simple: 'We keep the boys stimulated and always give them challenges; then they forget to be naughty.' This is easier than it might sound:

*'I'd like you to post this for me. Do you think you could get to the post box and back in three minutes? I'll time you.'*

With a little imagination on an adult's part, unpleasant, dull or 'uncool' activity can be reframed as exciting or challenging:

*The boys' bedroom needs tidying. They like playing soldiers, so their mother turns the task into an army game. The 'bunkroom inspection' will be carried out by the 'sergeant major' in ten minutes. The boys rush upstairs and tidy madly. After ten minutes their mother calls up in her best sergeant major voice and stomps slowly up the stairs. They stand to attention while she checks the room. Needless to say, they pass the inspection.*

*The youth worker spots a sweet on the floor at one end of the table-tennis table. It looks as though at any minute the player at that end will squash it. The adult motions to a boy who is waiting to play. 'I've got a dangerous job for you,' he whispers. The boy's ears perk up. 'Do you see that sweet at this end of the table?' he continues, pointing to it.*

*'Could you swoop in and pick it up without getting run over?'*

*The next time the table-tennis ball goes wide, the boy runs and picks up the sweet, then returns beaming to the youth worker. 'I knew you could do it!' he said. 'Put it in the bin.' The boy does.*

When one of my nephews didn't like what he had been given to eat, I told him about the game I had played when eating baked beans as a child: my plate was a swimming pool, the beans were people and I was a giant who came and ate them all up. Months later he reminded me of the story and explained a variation he had invented. He would think of someone he didn't like, imagine they were the food he wasn't keen on, spear them with his fork, pop them in his mouth and gobble them up.

> How can a grown-up get a boy upstairs to bed?
>
> *Say they'll race him to the top of the stairs (but they should make sure they let the boy win).*
>
> Matthew, aged 10

Boys can be encouraged into areas that they might normally shy away from by choosing boy-friendly ways of presenting them.

*Previous youth club discos had been pretty dismal, with girls dancing in small groups while boys watched from the side, wandered in and out, chased around and slid on the floor. A couple of months before the next disco was scheduled, the youth worker heard about a street dance teacher, so decided to offer some street dance classes. It turned out to be mostly boys that came, and the class was taught a series of moves that included jumps, spins and press-ups. The investment paid off: at the next disco both boys and girls were dancing. Two of the boys went to the centre of the dance floor and competed with each other, using every move they had learnt, plus a few they made up. Before long they were encircled by girls and boys clapping and chanting their names. By the end of the evening everyone was on the dance floor and the youth worker deemed the event a success.*

Antics that may be perceived as bad behaviour are often simply boys being imaginative. Adults can pick up on this in order to move things in the direction they want.

*On a camping trip the children are erecting the tents. One of the boys notices that the fibre ribs of the tent make an excellent fishing rod, and pretends to catch a huge fish.*

Instead of:    'For heaven's sake stop messing around with the tent poles!'

say:         *'Looks like you're going to land a couple of whoppers there. You're going to have to get that tent up quickly so we can cook them for tea.'*

When boys do not finding life interesting enough, they often create their own excitement by playing up. Some boys enjoy a battle with their peers or parents, seeing it as a challenge. The game is to provoke a fight, then win it. Don't fall into the double trap of first allowing them to wind you up and then trying to win the battle! If you don't get sucked in, they'll give up and find something more interesting to do.

### Use humour to get boys on side

Boys are mischievous; they like the rude and the ridiculous; they like to have fun. Adults can use humour to entertain, motivate or distract them.

To the boy who goes into a grump:

*'Hey, that's not a grump!' If you are going to do a grump, do it properly.'* The adult pulls a grumpy face and the boy can't help grinning.

*The youth worker has put some new posters up at different angles round the walls. Wanting a bit of attention, some boys start taking them down. Tongue in cheek, the youth worker says, 'Do you realise I've spent the whole afternoon putting those up with a spirit level?'*

*The boys mock the angles of the posters, and others join in the laughter. With a straight face the youth worker says, 'I'm sure you couldn't do any better!'*

*The boys rise to the challenge by putting up the posters they have taken down and repositioning all the others.*

Like their energy, boys' humour is sometimes seen as inappropriate or immature. Appropriateness, and timing, can be taught.

Boys study humour wherever they find it, and fathers in particular can have a great influence on the way boys use it, since their sons will inevitably copy them.

If adults exemplify playful constructive humour, then this will rub off on the boys around them. With age, the boys and their humour will gradually mature, but in the meantime it's easiest just to drop down to their level and have fun!

> *How do you kill a circus?*
> *Go for the juggler!*

---

### WHAT MAKES BOYS LAUGH

**5 years**   slapstick, visual/physical, funny noises

**7 years**   rude things, toilet humour, zany humour

**9 years**   jokes and joke books ('knock knock', 'doctor doctor', 'what did the x say to the y?', 'what do you get if you cross x with y?')

**11 years**  destruction, practical jokes, simple word-play, swear words, rudeness, gory things, funny stories

**13 years**  genitals, physical attributes, personal comments

**15 years**  sexual innuendo, irony, banter

---

Beware of using humour that boys aren't yet ready for. For example, older boys enjoy banter and it can be a great way of getting on with teenagers, but younger boys may not be able to follow what's being said. There is a very fine line between banter and sarcasm, and sarcasm can leave the victim feeling confused or hurt.

*Kieran took up karate when he was seven. He enjoyed it and practised hard. By the time he was ten he was near the top of the class and the teachers treated him as a senior student, someone who should know what's what. Then one day he came home from a class and announced that he wanted to give up – the teachers, he said, made fun of him when he made mistakes and he did not like being laughed at. His parents explained that because he was one of the higher grades, his teachers were using humour to tease him as they might an older person – it was a compliment and they meant no harm. Kieran was not persuaded; he did not go back.*

### *Set boys up to succeed*

It is easy to inadvertently set boys up to fail by expecting things of them that they are not easily able to do at a particular stage of development. Boys are generally less dextrous than girls of the same age, so a boy might need Velcro shoe fastenings for longer than his sister, find it easier to pull on a tracksuit than fiddle with zips and buttons, or prefer a fat crayon for drawing. On the other hand, a boy who finds it hard to use a needle and thread might be fascinated by – and able to use – a sewing machine. Rather than expecting all children to be capable of the same thing at the same age, be aware of differences and watch out for readiness. Once a boy is physically and mentally ready, he will pick up a new skill very quickly.

Allowing boys to pursue what interests them is a good way of channelling their energy, and they need to be able to work through their interests at their own pace. An interest may last a lifetime, or may be temporary. Be careful not to impose preconceived timescales onto boys.

*When Martin was nine years old, his parents told him that he was too old for dressing up and playing monsters, calling these activities 'babyish'. Martin stopped these games in the house, but behaved badly and was often rude and disobedient. His friend across the road was only seven, so when Martin played at his house, monsters and dressing up were considered normal. Over the next few years the two boys spent hours at the younger one's house playing imaginary games together. Martin felt comfortable there, and was always polite and co-operative. As they grew older, the boys' games and interests gradually changed. As teenagers they both developed an interesting sense of style, which served them well when they turned their attention to attracting girls.*

Sometimes boys' behaviour simply reflects the situation they find themselves in. If you find yourself persistently telling boys off, it is worth asking what about the situation might be provoking the behaviour, and what could be changed to prevent it. Asking boy's to sit quietly at a children's birthday party is unlikely to be successful; waking up to snow and telling boys to wait until after school to play in it will cause stress all round.

*All youth club members were expected to help set out the equipment at the beginning of the session. As soon as the cupboard was open, the boys would get the balls out and start playing basketball or football. When they were asked to stop and help set up, they just threw the ball to one another to avoid handing it over to an adult.*

*The youth workers found themselves getting increasingly irritated at the boys' lack of co-operation. When they analysed the situation, they realised that the problem was not the boys' attitude, but that the boys had access to the balls at the beginning of the session.*

*The following week the balls were removed from the cupboard before the club members arrived and only given to them once everything had been put out. The equipment was set up quickly and boys and girls were equally helpful.*

Steve Biddulph points out in *Raising Boys* that when boys run around and make a lot of noise this can be an anxiety response:

*There seems to be a built-in gender difference. If girls are anxious in a group setting they tend to cower and be quiet, whereas boys respond by running about, making a lot of noise. This has mistakenly been seen as 'dominating the space' in nursery schools and so on. However it is actually an anxiety response. Schools that are very good at engaging boys in interesting and concrete activities (such as Montessori schools where there is a lot of structural work with blocks, shapes, beads and so on) do not experience this gender difference in children's behaviour.*

Food additives can also affect behaviour. I heard of a youth club where they noticed members becoming 'hyper' after buying sweets from the tuck-shop. They made a point of buying sweets with fewer additives and the children became much calmer.

## Reading and writing

Parents and teachers despair at many boys' lack of interest in reading and writing. If you want a boy to read, then he needs reading matter that engages him. If a boy is interested in sharks, give him information about sharks; if he enjoys telling jokes, make sure there is a joke book on the shelf. There is a list of books that boys enjoy on page 198. Many boys initially find reading too slow and tedious – it's not fun, they feel unable, and the reward is not worth the effort. Adults can show boys the pleasure of books by reading to them; it's a great opportunity to be close and have a shared experience. By reading to a boy, you can introduce him to vocabulary and concepts years before he might access them on his own. When is a boy too old to be read to? When he takes the book out of your hand and says he would prefer to read it himself.

*'No way is poetry girlish. My mum bought me a book of poems written by a black rapper. It's brilliant.'* [5]

---

**THE 'COOL' READING RAP**

*If you really want your son to read*
*Get him the sort of book*
*Some parents don't seem to see.*
*It's all about image and being cool*
*And a lot depends on what you read at school.*
*Bugulugs Bum Thief*
*Goosebumps*
*Point Crime*
*Paul Jennings*
*The list goes on.*
*At least they are not glued*
*To a Nintendo playing Donkey Kong.*
*So take my advice*
*And you'll feel quite proud*
*Please don't make them read aloud.*
*If you do*
*They'll quit reading like a flash*
*And your reading scheme*
*Will fall down with a crash.*
*So if you take my tips*
*And do everything right*
*Your son could be reading*
*By tonight!*

Robert Chaseling, aged 11 [6]

---

Many boys do not like writing because initially they find it awkward to hold a slim writing implement, hard to form letters and tiring to write. Boys' handwriting is typically untidier than girls and criticism leads them to conclude that writing is a thankless task. Left to their own devices, boys often lie on the floor and use fat pens on large surfaces. Allowing them to do this makes writing and drawing an enjoyable activity. To improve boys' dexterity, encourage them to make things out of plasticine, to use scissors, to play with construction kits, and give them things they can take apart and then try to put back together.

If you start from where boys are, they will often allow you to take them in the direction you want. A primary school teacher was looking for ways to encourage a boy with dyslexia to write. He loved dinosaurs, so she cut paper into the shape of dinosaurs for him to write in. He was delighted by the dinosaur templates and filled each one with relative ease. Two weeks later, when offered a fresh template, he informed his teacher: 'I'm too big for that now. I'd like some proper paper.'

Author Alan Gibbons uses boys' interest in football and playstation games to get them reading and exploring deeper issues. In *The Legendeer Trilogy* the hero becomes a character in his playstation games taking part in a world of myth and legend. *Julie and Me ... and Michael Owen Makes Three* is the diary – both humorous and moving – of a football mad, love-sick teenager whose parents are separating.

When helping a boy with his homework, it is important to differentiate between the content of what he has been asked to do and the writing itself. Many boys can easily get their thoughts out by talking, but find it hard to write them down. Parents or siblings can help by asking the boy to talk out his ideas, while themselves making simple notes to remind him of what he said. He can then copy or enlarge on these himself. By separating the activity of writing from the content, he is able to use his creative mind freely without being discouraged by having to write it down. For longer projects it is worth explaining that only the final draft requires a high standard of presentation. Boys with messy handwriting often prefer to use a computer.

If boys read a lot and have a good visual memory, they are likely to spell well; but otherwise they may have difficulties. Bored or daunted by the school spelling list, boys may prefer to spell long words that they like the sound of (brontosaurus, gastronomic, dodecahedron). Challenging a boy to spell something backwards means he has to visualise the word. Boys who cannot be bothered to open a traditional dictionary may find an electronic dictionary much more attractive.

Boys can show surprising ability when they see reading or writing as a means to an end that interests them.

*The craze was Pokémon – a Japanese cartoon featuring collectable fighting monsters. At eight and ten years old, the two brothers were not keen on schoolwork and would rather be playing; they spent their pocket money on Pokémon trading cards, and their spare time playing games based on the cartoon. One day their father noticed they had been quiet upstairs for a suspiciously long time, so went to check what they were up to. He found them at a desk, with piles of scrap paper in front of them. On each piece they had drawn an invented monster, and beneath it had neatly written a name and information to describe its characteristics. Each heading was underlined and had a colon placed after it. With care, imagination and perfect presentation the boys had produced their own pack of Pokémon cards.*

## Create a good relationship with school

Set boys up to succeed by making the effort to build a good relationship with school. Doing this early on makes communication easier if a boy later has any problems at school. One way to build a good relationship is to offer to help the school in some way: most schools value parental support and boys benefit hugely from seeing fathers as well as mothers getting involved.

You can build positive relations with individual teachers by staying in touch and telling them how your son is doing. This is relatively easy when the boy is young as he is likely to have one teacher and is often picked up from school by a parent. It becomes harder when there are different teachers for each subject and the boy makes his own way to and from school. Communication may have to be by letter, e-mail or telephone; make sure it always has a positive tone, and problems are addressed while they are still minor.

Bear in mind that a teacher typically has 30 children in a

class and at secondary school may be teaching around 200 different pupils in a week. Children often behave differently at home and at school, and teachers respond to what they are presented with, so make sure you give them relevant information about your son.

Some teachers find boys harder to teach than girls and this can rub off in the way they relate to a boy and describe him to his parents. When discussing your son's progress or behaviour, both parties need to be as specific as possible. If what you are being told is not specific, ask questions to clarify, then summarise your understanding of any problems. Tell teachers what they do that your son responds well to: this will encourage them to do more of the same.

When arranging a meeting with a teacher, consider whether it would be helpful for the boy to attend. Sometimes it may be better to discuss a problem in his absence; at other times it may be useful for him to be included. One solution might be to have a frank conversation between adults first, where both sides have the opportunity to raise concerns that they may not want the boy to hear, then have a separate meeting with all three parties later. Such a meeting should not dwell on the problem, but focus on finding workable solutions to it, concentrating on facts and exploring options. Everyone should leave such a meeting with their honour intact: avoid showing up your son in front of his teacher, or showing up a teacher in front of him.

CHAPTER SUMMARY

# Channelling Boys' Energy

### Give boys opportunities to express their physical energy
- Get them outside as often as possible
- Allow energetic and imaginative activities in certain indoor areas
- Encourage involvement in physical pursuits
- Teach self-discipline through play fighting

### Keep boys stimulated and challenged
- Recognise the imaginary worlds that they often inhabit
- Turn unpleasant tasks into games or challenges
- Present activities in boy-friendly ways

### Use humour to get boys on side
- Humour can motivate, distract and entertain
- Adapt your humour to the age of the boys
- Banter works, but be careful with sarcasm

### Set boys up to succeed
- Make expectations appropriate to a boy's stage of development
- Give boys opportunities to do what interests them
- Look out for and remove external triggers for poor behaviour
- Create a good relationship with school

NOTEBOOK

Think of ways you can give boys opportunities to express their physical energy.

Consider the interests of individual boys. How can you use these interests to channel their energy?

When do you find boys' energy too much? What could you do or say to channel their energy at these times?

Think of ways you can offer boys challenges.

You want a boy to do his homework. How could you make this sound exciting?

Think of examples of when you have used or could use humour to channel boys' energy.

When does boys' humour wind you up? How could you respond to it differently?

Are there any sarcastic phrases that you use regularly? What could you say instead?

Can you think of any situation where boys' bad behaviour might be caused or made worse by something external? How could this be avoided?

**About Our Boys**

## Chapter 3

# Boundaries and Discipline

*Good discipline contains a boy and his energy, providing a
sense of physical and emotional security he needs in order
to learn the larger lessons of self-control and moral
behaviour.*

Kindlon and Thompson, *Raising Cain*

In the plenary session of a conference about boys,[1] a man in
the audience concluded:

*Today we have learned that boys are wired up to push
boundaries – that is their job. An adult's job is to hold those
boundaries firm.*

A boundary is the line between acceptable and unacceptable
behaviour. As natural explorers and risk-takers, boys often
go to the very limit, and so it is essential that they know
what the limits are. If boundaries are weak or absent, the
boys receive no guidance as to what is acceptable and what
is not. Boys need boundaries; they also want boundaries.
Clear boundaries, firmly held, make boys feel safe and
cared for.

Since most boys instinctively test boundaries, the harder
they push, the firmer (but not tighter) those boundaries
should be. Part of the purpose of boundaries is to provide
boys with something to push against, so don't be surprised
or angry when they do just that!

When a boy says, 'Do I have to?' he usually means, 'I am honour-bound to resist, but if you tell me I have to then I will'. If the adult answers with a simple 'Yes', the boy can breathe a sigh of relief and do what he has been asked to without feeling obliged to resist further.

When my son was young, he resisted his job of clearing the table but, once he was doing it, would often skip to and from the kitchen. As a teenager he left his bike tyre unrepaired for over a month; when we finally said 'no lifts until your bike is working', we heard him singing in the garage as he repaired it. His mind resisted the tasks, but his body, and perhaps his soul, embraced them.

Used well, discipline builds character and encourages responsibility; used badly, it creates resentment and teaches brutality. Boundaries and discipline require firmness and consistency, and although anger can sometimes be constructive, a light touch often gets the message across more effectively.

---

**Boys respond best to adults who are:**
*Firm, Fair & Fun*

---

Incorporating these characteristics into the way you deal with boys is likely to maximise co-operation and minimise conflict.

## To maintain boundaries:

- Ensure boys know what the boundaries are
- Apply them fairly and consistently
- Use positive language to reinforce them
- Give sanctions that are consequences of behaviour and limited in time
- Keep communication channels open

### *Ensure boys know what the boundaries are*

Boys need to know the limits of acceptable behaviour and what sanctions apply should those limits be broken. In order to make sure boys are clear about where they stand, rules and sanctions should be clearly defined.

If boundaries are constantly expressed in the negative – 'No...' or 'Don't...' – boys can feel controlled and constrained, and react by rebelling. A constant 'no' is literally antagonistic and gives the message 'we are against one another'; it is no surprise, then, when boys fight against this. Boundaries are more effective when phrased positively, for example:

*'Everyone helps with the clearing up.'*
*'Be back by 6.00 p.m.'*
*'Ball games on the grass.'*

Occasionally a boundary needs to be stated in the negative in order to be explicit, for example:

*'No hitting.'*

Displaying rules prominently ensures they are absorbed even if they are not consciously read. This even applies to non-readers: if rules are written up and pointed out clearly to young children, possibly with a picture for each rule, they will be able to tell you what each rule says even though they cannot read. Having rules written down or displayed makes the rules independent of the adult enforcing them, so a boy is less likely to take it personally when he is reminded of one (and equally the adult need not take it personally if a boy oversteps a boundary). As years go by, some rules will be developed and some will be removed. Here is an example of some youth club rules.

---

### Youth Club Rules

RESPECT EACH OTHER

- Look after each other
- Take turns
- Use respectful language

RESPECT THE BUILDING AND EQUIPMENT

- Put litter in the bin
- Clear up if you make a mess
- Don't sit or stand on the games tables
- Leave your bikes outside
- Play indoor football with a soft ball

**Sanctions**

Yellow Card – warning

2 Yellow Cards – 1 week ban

Red Card – 2 week ban

---

Some boundaries will be set in stone, others may be negotiable; it helps boys if they are told which is which and why.

Club members have asked if a boisterous game can be organised.

Adult: *'There are a lot of people here tonight and the atmosphere is a bit wild. I don't want to play that game in case someone gets hurt. We'll do it on a night when there are fewer people and it's calmer.'*

Where there is room for negotiation, show boys that they are most likely to get their way when they are polite and reasonable:

*The family has a rule of one hour's television a day. The boy comes back from school in a bad mood and switches on the TV. His mother reminds him of the one-hour rule and asks if that is the viewing he had planned for the day. He doesn't respond and she leaves him. When she hears the end of the programme, she comes back and repeats her question. He remembers his favourite programme is on later that night, and flies into a rage because there isn't enough TV time left that day to watch it.*

*The mother might say something like: 'It seems like you've had a bad day, but shouting like that is not going to help you watch your programme. Let's switch the TV off and talk this through.' Once the TV is off she says, 'I know it's your favourite programme. And the rule is one hour's TV a day. Have a think, to see if you can suggest a way round this. A tip though – I'm likely to be more open to your ideas if you are calm and polite.'*

*With a younger boy she might help him think the problem through; with an older one she might ask him to come back to her with a suggestion. For the purposes of this example, let's suppose they agree to take the extra time off the following day's viewing, and avoid the situation in future by putting a list of chosen viewing next to the TV each week.*
[For more on problem solving, see Chapter 6.]

Boundaries will change as a boy gets older, and it is important to recognise when he is ready for greater freedom and responsibility. Within a family it is often easiest to apply the same boundaries to all the children, and where these boundaries incorporate family values it is right to do so. In areas relating to freedom or supervision, the boundary is likely to be related to age: a five-year-old should not expect to go to bed at the same time as his eleven-year-old brother, and the eleven-year-old should not expect the five-year-old to do as many jobs around the house as he does!

### Apply boundaries fairly and consistently

If a boundary is applied consistently, then it is seen as a firm boundary and boys will accept it; if it is applied inconsistently, they perceive it as flexible and worth testing at every opportunity. It is much better to have firm boundaries that are relaxed on special occasions, than flexible boundaries that are suddenly tightened up when the adult has had enough.

Every adult will have a slightly different view of what is and is not acceptable, so it is worth the adults discussing and agreeing boundaries to avoid confusion. Sometimes the boundaries will differ with different people or in different places: for example, a higher level of noise is acceptable for one adult or situation than another; or toy guns may be allowed in the house but not on the street. Make sure boys are clear about such differences.

I once asked a teenage boy what was the most important thing adults needed to know about boys. His answer was, 'Boys need space'.

---

**Boys need space**

---

He explained that boys need to be given a little time and space to take on what they have been asked to do, and to decide for themselves to do it. This is called 'take-up time'. When you ask a boy to do something, give him some take-up time by looking away, saying nothing, occupying yourself with something else, or leaving the room. If the boy feels he has space, he may well comply; if he feels controlled, mistrusted or nagged, he might feel obliged to rebel. Giving the boy space also gives him the message that the adult is confident that he will do what he has been asked.

Many boys regard breaking boundaries as a game; part of the game is seeing if they can get away with it. When they are caught, most will take it as a 'fair cop', as long as they are treated respectfully. However, if they are blamed for something they haven't done, the sense of injustice causes resentment. This is especially so with boys who often do break the rules, since they feel picked on and so obliged to defend themselves.

Boys are sensitive to adults apparently favouring girls. Girls and boys tend to push boundaries in different ways. Often a girl will subtly step outside a boundary and her behaviour draws little attention. A boy, on the other hand, tends to be more 'in your face': it is often because of boys' behaviour that the boundary is drawn in the first place; but once a boundary has been set, it is important that it be seen to apply to both girls and boys:

*A series of circus skills workshops had been set up to run for the hour before youth club. The response to the first workshop had been good. The interest dropped off during the second session: the same number came, but while one group practised to improve their skill, another group chatted and messed about. The instructor and youth worker made a ground rule that in future sessions anyone who came should spend the time practising circus skills.*

*For the third session fewer youngsters came and the atmosphere was more productive. The youth worker noticed two boys sitting chatting. He went up to them and reminded them of the ground rule that anyone attending the workshop should be doing circus skills.*

*'So what is it to be, boys,' he asked with a smile, 'practise circus skills, or come back at seven for youth club?'*

*He didn't get an immediate response to his question. One boy looked surly and said, 'It's not fair. You always pick on me!'*

*The youth worker was not aware that he did, but recognised this was how the boy saw things, so he called to a girl who was sitting watching the others practising: 'Lucy, the rule is if you are here you practise circus skills. Do you want to join in or come back at seven for youth club?'*

*Lucy thought for a moment: 'I'll come back later,' and she got up to leave.*

*He turned to the two boys. 'So what is it to be, boys,' he repeated, 'practise circus skills, or come back at seven?'*

*The boys looked slightly surprised at Lucy's departure, and the youth worker, knowing that they both fancied her, expected them to follow. To his surprise, both opted to stay. They immediately joined in the activity and after ten minutes' practice were calling him over to admire their new skills.*

Part of fairness is being seen not to hold a grudge, so adults should make a point of dropping the issue after telling boys off. Sometimes it is worth saying something that makes it clear you have moved on.

*'O.K. Telling off over.'*

*'That's that dealt with. Now, how are you getting on with your canoeing?'*

*'Well, now you know how I feel about that. [pause] Anyway, I'm pleased I ran into you because I heard you had done well in your chess tournament and I wanted to congratulate you.'*

There will be occasions when fairness and consistency have

to be overridden by doing what works best in particular circumstances. Adults must use their own judgment in such cases. It often works to explain your reasoning.

With a teenage boy who doesn't usually put much effort into schoolwork:

Boy: *'I need some money for my haircut – will you give me some?'*

Normally: *'Your haircuts come out of your monthly allowance. If you have run out of money, your hair will have to wait till next month.'*

Occasionally: *'Normally I would say your hair cut will have to wait till you get next month's allowance. On this occasion I've been so impressed at the amount of effort you put into your school project work that I'll pay for your haircut as a 'well done'.'*

To a boy complaining his older sister has been favoured:

*'Yes, your sister was allowed in later than you at this age. There were two reasons for that – she got her homework done before she went out, and she got back at the time we agreed. When you can do that, you'll be allowed out later too.'*

Some events have their own logic:

*There was a crash. Fourteen-year-old Steven ran in, as white as a sheet. 'It was me,' he gasped. 'I broke the window!'*

*The adult started issuing instructions to Steven and his*

*friends. One boy should clear up the broken glass, another find cardboard and tape to cover the hole, a third run across the road and ask a neighbour who installs windows to come over and give advice.*

*Steven's friends were puzzled by this reaction and asked the adult: 'Why aren't you angry with Steven? He broke the window. You yell at us for much less than that.'*

*The adult acknowledged this was true, but pointed out that Steven was the boy who usually said, 'It wasn't me!' On this occasion not only had he admitted to breaking the window, but was clearly very sorry he had; he didn't need her to be angry. The boys concurred and went off to do the things they had been asked.*

*The neighbour arrived, offered to fit a new glazed unit at cost, and estimated it would be £30. When everything was cleared up, the adult had another word with Steven. Since he had broken the window, he would be expected to pay for the new one. Steven proposed a deal: he would pay £5 a week as long as his parents were not told of the incident.*

*The deal was struck and for the next six weeks Steven came round after he had received payment for his paper round and handed over the £5 he owed.*

Whether and when you choose to tell a boy's parents about what he has been up to can be sensitive, and will depend on the age of the boy, the seriousness of the incident, and his reaction to it. When deciding, consider the relationship of trust both between you and the parent and between you and the boy. If you decide the parents need to know, then you may want to warn the boy you are going to tell them. He is

likely to appreciate you being up front with him and giving
him the opportunity to tell them his side of the story.

### Use positive language to reinforce boundaries

The nature of boys is that they will overstep boundaries, so
adults should not take their actions personally, but remind
them of the boundary with clear, positive and impersonal
language.

Instead of: 'I'm sick to death of having to tell you to go to
bed!'

say: *'Your bedtime is nine o'clock.'*

Instead of: 'Stop being so selfish, Paul. Give Amber a
turn!'

say: *'Paul, it's Amber's turn.'*

It is not just language that needs to be positive, but also the
tone of voice. Boys respond best to a tone that is firm yet
not harsh. Occasional anger can be effective, giving boys
the message that they have seriously overstepped the mark
this time. But if an adult frequently sounds angry, then boys
stop taking any notice, and the anger becomes something to
be endured, or even a source of amusement.

Children pick up on whether you appear to mean what you
say; if you don't seem to, they pay little attention. Faced
with boys ignoring what I have asked them to do, I have
noticed my voice 'shift gear' as I connect with what I want.
Then, even though I might be using the same words, I
sound as though I mean it and the boys do what I ask.

Listen to yourself when you 'connect' and see if you can work out what is happening. You may have taken a deeper breath, which gives the voice more authority.

*The youth worker went into the hall and saw sweet papers all over the floor. She held out the bin in front of her and called out above the noise, 'Everyone put five pieces of litter in the bin!' Her tone was friendly but purposeful and she kept repeating the request until everyone got the message. Three minutes later the floor was clean.*

Boys sometimes accuse adults of noticing what they do wrong but not what they do right. Boys who get attention only when they behave badly may use bad behaviour as an attention-seeking strategy. Boys need to experience a pay-off from sticking to the rules; adults can provide this by acknowledging when they stay within the boundaries that have been set.

*'Thank you for taking turns, Paul.'*
*'It's good to see you back at the time we agreed.'*
*'It's great that you get your homework done with no fuss.'*
*'I noticed you looking out for Jim. That was kind.'*
*'Everyone worked hard to make that a success. I was really impressed.'*

As boys move towards teenagehood, they become sensitive to sarcasm and double meanings, so do make sure any acknowledgement is sincere. Keeping it low-key can avoid embarrassment on their part. At this age many boys like to portray a cool image and could feel shown up if their peers heard them praised for keeping within the boundaries. A useful guideline is to praise a group of boys publicly, but individual boys privately. Sometimes a positive gesture is enough – such as a thumbs-up or a high-five.

## The use of questions

Adults often ask questions in the hope of getting to the bottom of a misdemeanour. But this can encourage defensiveness and lying if the question implies blame.

| Blame Question | Defensive Response |
|---|---|
| *'Who did this?'* | *'It wasn't me!'* |
| *'What are you doing?'* | *'Nothing.'* |
| *'Why did you do that?'* | *'Because I did.'* |

It is more effective to replace such questions with statements or expectations.

Instead of:  'Who did this?'

say:       *'I'd like this mess cleared up.'*

or:        *'I'd like whoever did this to be man enough to own up.'*

Instead of:  'Why did you do that?'

say:       *'You know that the rule is x, so the sanction for doing this is y.'*

If you want a truthful response to a question, use a tone of voice that makes it clear that it is a sincere enquiry. It can also help to preface the question with something that shows your intention is positive.

Instead of:  'What are you doing?'

say:          *'You sound like you're having a good time.*
              *What are you doing?'*

Instead of:   'How could you do something like that?'
say:          *'It's not like you to do something like that.*
              *What's the matter?'*

These questions imply that the adult is seeing the best in the boy, so he is more likely to respond well to them.

### *Sanctions and consequences*

When boundaries are exceeded, then sanctions usually apply. The purpose of sanctions is not, as is often imagined, to punish, but to teach self-discipline and encourage social and moral behaviour in future. Sanctions should be chosen with this in mind.

Parenthood brings with it a range of feelings that for many are more extreme than they have experienced before: on the negative side these include exhaustion, irritation, frustration, anger, outrage and sometimes jealousy or despair. When a child provokes such deep reactions, parents sometimes do or say something they later regret. It is worth taking a few seconds to step back from the situation before doing or saying anything. Those few seconds will often make the difference between confrontation and co-operation.

> *Don't just say something; stand there.*
> Faber and Mazlish

Boys respond best to a non-confrontational approach to discipline, and to being rebuked privately. Public reprimand leaves them smarting with humiliation and often evokes a 'couldn't care less' response in order to save face. Discipline should be fair, appropriate to the circumstances, consistently applied and respectful.

---

**Discipline should be:**
**Fair✧Appropriate✧Consistent✧Respectful**

---

In order that the boy actively learns from the situation, select sanctions that are consequences rather than punishments.

*If he makes a mess, he clears it up.*

*If he is five minutes late, he comes in five minutes early next time.*

*If he breaks something, he apologises / mends it / pays for it.*

*If he doesn't put his clothes in the wash basket, they don't get washed.*

It sometimes takes more thought and supervision to apply 'consequences' than punishments. But as boys learn from this approach, they will become more responsible about what they choose to do, so it is likely that less time will have to be spent on discipline in the long run. The appropriateness of the consequence will vary with age. Since the consequence itself teaches the boy a lesson, there is no need for lectures.

*A boy refuses to help unload the shopping. Later he asks for a lift.*

Instead of:    'You just take, take, take! You won't help me when I ask, but as soon as you want a lift it's all smiles and niceness. I just feel taken for granted!'

say (calmly):   *'You didn't feel like helping me out earlier. I don't feel like helping you out now.'*

In the example above, it is instructive for the boy to have to wait a little to see the consequences of his actions, but often it is better for him to be forewarned. Warnings, however, can easily turn into threats and boys soon learn whether or not to heed them. Beware of using threats you are unlikely to carry out; instead, adapt expectations, boundaries and consequences to the age of the child, then follow through on the consequences. When my son was two, I often took him to a children's playground in the park near our house. One day, when I told him it was time to leave, he refused to come, so I told him I would go without him. I had no intention of doing so, but went to the other side of the playground so he would think that I had. I came back expecting him to be ready to do what I asked. Instead, he was nowhere to be seen. Panic-stricken, I searched the playground, then went out into the park to look for him. I spotted him with a couple, walking in my direction. They had found him walking to the gates of the park. He had taken me at my word, assumed I had left the playground without him, and set out for home on his own. Using the threat to frighten him had only made the situation worse.

The consequence I had threatened my son with when he was two was perfectly appropriate when he was twelve, and my husband used it to teach a lesson about keeping agreements. He had taken our son and a friend into town, about three miles away, and asked them to meet him back at the car at a certain time. If they were not there, he warned them, he would go without them and they would have to walk home. I don't think they believed him; but, in any case, they were not back at the agreed time and found the car gone. An hour or so later they arrived home. The consequence of their lateness was a three-mile walk, and they learnt that when this father said something, he meant it. An unexpected by-product of the episode was discovering an independence they did not have before, and from then on they often asked if they could walk home for fun.

---

**Sanctions should be:**

✧

**A consequence of the misdemeanour**

✧

**Appropriate to the boys' maturity**

✧

**Limited in time**

---

It is easy to make the mistake of imposing sanctions that last longer than necessary for the boy to learn the required lesson. If the punishment outweighs the crime, it will seem unjust to the boy, and any initial remorse will quickly be replaced by resentment. The longer the sanction is in place, the more the resentment will grow. If the boy sees no honourable way out, then, to avoid the humiliation of surrender and to keep his pride intact, he will cut off and dig himself in. Instead of the punishment encouraging better behaviour, it can result in an extended stand-off and worse behaviour.

In *Raising Cain*, Kindlon and Thompson relate the story of a thirteen-year-old boy who was not doing as well as he should at school: he was rude and insolent at home, and had been playing truant. Each time he did something wrong his parents withdrew some of his privileges. When all his privileges had been withdrawn – TV, going out, time with friends, use of the computer and the phone – his behaviour did not improve, in fact it worsened, so they resorted to removing things from his room – his stereo, his dartboard, his posters and so on. He was eventually left with a bed, a desk and a chair. None of this improved his behaviour, but in the meantime all communication between him and his parents had broken down.

Family therapist Ken Rutter tells of a teenage girl whose parents used the sanction of grounding so liberally that when all the weeks of grounding were added together their daughter wouldn't have left the house until she was eighteen. Since this was impracticable, the sanction was largely ignored by all parties, rendering it ineffective.

Whether the difference in outcomes of these two stories reflects the gender of the teenager or is simply coincidental, I don't know; boys often seem to be punished more harshly than girls. But both of these stories illustrate the danger of sanctions that go on for too long. Limiting the period of the sanction gives the boy an incentive to start behaving; it also makes that sanction available for the adult to use again if needed.

Instead of:   'I knew I couldn't trust you with that sword! Give it to me. I'm not having you play with swords in this house again!'

say:   *'If you hit your sister with the sword, I will put it away.'*

or:   *'You hit your sister with the sword, so I am putting it away until tomorrow.'*

Instead of:   'What kind of time do you call this? We've been worried sick about you. That's it, no more going out with your friends – you are grounded until the end of term!'

say:   *'You are an hour late, so you may not go out with your friends tomorrow. The next time you are given a time to be in, make sure you stick to it.'*

Instead of:   'We don't want your kind in this club. Go away and don't come back.'

say:   *'I'm giving you a one-week ban from the club. If you're prepared to stick to the rules, you will be welcome back after that.'*

Instead of:   'Go to your room, and don't come down until
dinner time!' (This is likely to result in a pretty
bad atmosphere at dinner.)

say:    *'Go up to your room until you've calmed
down.' (Once he seems to have calmed down,
the adult might go up and have a quiet talk
with him.)*

Different sanctions will work at different times and with
different individuals. When my son was a teenager, he went
through a really cantankerous phase for a few months, when
he didn't want to do what he was asked, thought school was
a waste of time and wouldn't do his homework. His catch-
phrase was, 'It's my life and I can do what I want with it.'
When I told him he couldn't go out, he just walked out of
the door. Since I could no longer physically prevent him, I
had to look for other strategies. The one thing he cared
about was skating, so when he refused to do his homework,
I put his skates in a place he wouldn't find them and told
him I would put them back when his homework was done.
He would mutter something about me being mean and evil
(this was not an insult, merely an admission of defeat), then
get on with his work.

Involving boys in making rules and choosing sanctions can
make it easier to get them to abide by them, and they often
suggest harsher penalties than an adult might have!

*When Lucan was six he went through a stage of being rude
and unco-operative, especially with women. For a few
months, even his grandparents wouldn't have him to stay*

*because they found him so unpleasant. Once it had been decided he could visit them again, Lucan's mother had a conversation with him. She'd like him to be polite, she didn't want to spend her time nagging him in front of other people, and she certainly didn't want another period when he wasn't welcome in her parents' house. Had Lucan any ideas on how they could make this work?*

*'If I was you, Mum,' the six-year-old replied, ' I'd stop my pocket money if I'm rude or I don't do what you say.'*

*And so the 'pocket money count' was born. If Lucan was rude or unco-operative, his mother would say, 'I'm going to start counting.' If his behaviour did not improve immediately, the counting began, and each number represented a penny off his pocket money at the end of the week. Onlookers were not aware of the significance of the counting, and it seldom went further than 'six'.*

*As Lucan grew older, the sanction was needed less often, but the 'exchange rate' increased. At ten years old he lost ten pence for each number, and at fourteen it increased to a pound. A warning was always given, and he could earn the money back by doing jobs around the house.*

It is possible to fall into the trap of not choosing the most appropriate sanction because it seems sacrosanct:

*A talented swimmer is taken to early morning coaching sessions by his stepmother. Resentful of his parents' divorce, the boy is often rude to her when they are alone together. Even though she knows he needs to train every day for an important championship, she tells him: 'If you*

*swear at me again today, I will not take you to swimming
tomorrow.'*

In this example the boy has to take responsibility for his
behaviour. If he chooses to continue swearing, he will either
have to miss his next training session or make other
arrangements to get there.

When selecting a sanction, be careful not to choose one that
causes a problem for you or for everyone else. For example,
if an outing is planned and a boy misbehaves prior to it, you
may rashly tell him he can't come, and then find you have to
stay behind to look after him. Before deciding, run through
a few checking questions in your head:

- Did he know this sanction would be applied?
- Is the sanction commensurate with his bad behaviour?
- Will his absence make it better or worse for the rest of
  the group?
- Are you creating a problem for yourself or anyone else
  by not taking him?
- Is this sanction likely to improve his behaviour in both
  the short and long run?
- Does he have a way of winning back this privilege?
- Would another sanction be more appropriate?

Sometimes adults need to consult each other before
choosing a course of action:

*The youth club was planning a weeklong residential trip.
They had been having problems with a boy named Mark,
whose behaviour seemed irrational and so possibly*

*dangerous. When Mark put his name down for the trip, the youth workers were dismayed, and one announced that if Mark was allowed to go, she would not be prepared to help. The adults talked the problem through and came up with a workable compromise. One of the youth workers would talk to Mark and explain that they were not sure he was able to control his behaviour and so had reservations about him coming on the trip. He had the two months before the trip to demonstrate whether he was able to control himself. If he showed he could, then he would be allowed on the trip; if he showed he couldn't, then he wouldn't.*

In a situation like the one above, make sure the boy is clear about what kind of behaviour you expect of him and what kind of behaviour will lead to his exclusion from the trip.

Beware of punishing a boy for something he has already been punished for elsewhere. I heard of a boy who was put on report at school. When his parents learnt of this they were so angry that they grounded him for the whole of the Easter holiday. Instead of the boy returning from the holiday refreshed, able to move on and start the new term with a positive attitude, he returned resentful, convinced that the whole world was against him.

If, over a period of time, a boy does not respond to sanctions, then it may be a sign that he is depressed. [For causes and symptoms of depression see page 150.] Such a boy is probably feeling hopeless, alone and lost. What he needs is love and reassurance. His attitude and behaviour, however, are more likely to provoke frustration and anger in adults, and it is all too easy to move into heavy discipline (which will be ineffective), or simply to give up on him. If depression is spotted early, then a change in circumstances or approach can nip it in the bud.

> When a depressed boy tells you he doesn't care, he is not being defiant; he is accurately describing his emotional state.

### Keep communication channels open

We need to encourage boys to be open and honest with us about what they get up to. If they receive heavy reprimands or sanctions when they do this, then they will stop telling us and we will not find out what is going on.

*A boy tells you about the pranks he and his friends got up to on the school bus, which included, writing on the seat and making fun of other pupils.*

Instead of: rebuking him severely for being a vandal and a bully

try: *explaining that what might seem like fun to him and his friends could be seen as vandalism and bullying, and say you want him to treat the bus and his fellow pupils with respect.*

The earlier story about the boy whose bedroom was stripped of possessions shows how communication can break down. It is often in such serious situations that sanctions need to be set aside in favour of talking things through. For example, you find out that a boy has been taking drugs: the obvious sanction for a parent might be to stop him leaving the house (so he doesn't have an opportunity to take more); for a youth worker the obvious sanction might be to stop him attending the club (so he can't be a bad influence on others). However, in these cases it is very important to keep communication open, and sane conversations about drugs may have a more positive effect on his future behaviour than sanctions. In such a case, the boy might be supported by tightening some boundaries – perhaps by reducing the length of time he goes out at any one time, or making sure his parents drop him off and pick him up from the club. He needs to know why he is being reined in, and that the boundaries will gradually be loosened as the adults are reassured by changes in his behaviour.

Taking time to find out what has gone on and to discuss values with boys develops character and responsibility:

*Nick's phone rang at 9 p.m. on Halloween. He was the parish clerk and Alan, a relatively new resident, was phoning him to report a group of boys who had come 'Trick or Treating'. Alan had given them some money, then one of them had thrown an egg at him. It wasn't the first time he'd had trouble from the local boys: over the last few months they had been looking in his windows and playing knock and run.*

*'Leave it with me,' responded Nick, 'My own son's thirteen, so I know a lot of the kids. I'll see what I can find out.'*

*The next day Nick had a word with some of the youngsters and their parents to establish what had gone on the night before. The kids were willing to tell him what had happened and to suggest who else might have done it, but no one would admit to being involved. It turned out that another egg had been thrown at an old lady's front door, and a firecracker had been thrown onto a doorstep and had gone off when the door was opened.*

*Nick explained the problem to a mother in whose house many of the teenage boys hung out. She was also committed to sorting it out and they sat in the lounge with half a dozen boys, discussing the rights and wrongs of what had happened the night before. Some boys felt it had gone too far, others thought it was a lot of fuss about nothing.*

*'Well,' said one, 'they deserved it!'*

*What, asked the adults, would make someone deserve being egged – especially someone who had just given you some money?*

*The boys exchanged glances, and then one spoke up: 'We've seen Alan watching porn through his window. And Mrs T is an old witch and swears at us when we're outside her house.'*
*According to the boys' code of morality, these acts made the victims fair game.*

*Nick and the mother pointed out that the boys shouldn't have been in Alan's garden to look through his window, and that it wasn't their job to punish people they disapproved of, even if those people hadn't treated them respectfully. Then fourteen-year old Josh spoke up: 'I threw the egg at the witch. I'll go and apologise.' And he got up and walked out.*

*Five minutes later he was back. Everyone was dying to know what happened. Did she come to the door? What did she say?*

*'Yes, she came to the door,' said Josh. 'I told her I had egged her front door yesterday and I apologised. She thanked me for apologising and that was it.'*

*His friends were dumb-founded and impressed.*

*The conversation moved on to Alan. Some of the boys admitted to being in the group that had knocked at his house, and to having spied through his windows earlier in the year. It was Ryan who had thrown the egg, they said. Ryan had been lying low since denying any involvement earlier in the day. So Nick went round to his house. He explained to Ryan that the others had admitted their involvement, and that Chris had already gone and apologised to the old lady. Ryan looked uncomfortable, then said, 'Oh all right, it was me that threw the egg. I didn't mean to throw it at him. I threw it at the door and it bounced off and landed on his chest.'*

*On hearing this, his mother told him she would take him up to apologise to Alan that minute. As he walked down the path Ryan hissed at Nick, 'And what about the firecracker? I think you'll find the person who did that is in your street. In fact, I think you'll find he is in your house!' And with this parting shot he followed his mother up to Alan's house.*

*Nick went home and found his son. 'Mike, did you have anything to do with the firecracker on the doorstep?'*

*A grin spread across the boy's face. 'I'll take that as a yes,' said the boy's father. 'It was a dangerous thing to do, and I'd like you to apologise to them for it.'*

*Mike was not happy with this idea, despite hearing that Josh and Ryan had been brave enough to apologise face to face. However, he agreed to apologise in writing and delivered the letter that evening.*

*The next October Nick and some of the parents warned the kids off eggs and firecrackers at Halloween, and the evening passed without incident.*

## Sex, Alcohol, Tobacco and Drugs

Some boundaries are easy to monitor, others are much harder. As boys grow they will be tempted by forbidden fruits, so adults need to give them values and knowledge that will allow them to make wise decisions as and when they need to.

In her commentary on the findings of the *Leading Lads* survey[2] of adolescent boys, Adrienne Katz expresses concern that adults are failing to provide boys with meaningful guidance about sex and drugs. Of the 1,344 boys surveyed, 4% had received most of their information about sex from their father, 11% from their mother, and 40% from school; the remaining 49% got most of their information from friends, girlfriends, TV, videos or magazines. Although the likelihood of boys taking drugs rises with age, useful guidance from parents declined as boys moved through adolescence. While 80% of the youngest teenagers in the sample said their parents gave them clear and helpful information about illegal drugs, this dropped with each year group, to 30% at nineteen years old.

Children become interested in the differences between boys and girls at a young age, and a good way to teach small boys what they need to know about sex is to answer any questions they ask. At three, four or five years old, they are likely to ask simple questions, to which they need factual answers appropriate to their level of understanding. Every time a boy receives a straight answer, it will add to his knowledge, show that it is all right to explore the topic, and keep that channel of communication open. If you don't think you are the right person to answer his questions, suggest a suitable adult for him to ask.

Questions still need answering as boys gets older, but sometimes they may be a bit near the bone. If a question is too personal, then you can make it clear you are happy to give information, but not to discuss your private life.

Teenagers get a lot of misinformation about sex from their friends, so it is vital that adults give boys of this age useful facts and guidance. Rather than waiting for the 'right moment' to have a serious talk, adults can pick up on comments or jokes that boys make, and use the opportunity to check out understanding and give additional information or insights. The use of the word 'gay' to insult a friend could prompt a discussion about sexuality. If boys' sexual banter implies that everyone should be sexually active, you could point out that there is often a disparity between what people say about sex and what is actually happening. If the language or concepts become disrespectful, explain the difference between joking and saying things that degrade others.

Boys don't just want to be given dire warnings about underage sex, sexually transmitted diseases and teenage pregnancy; they also want to know about relationships and how to deal with their feelings. Men can reassure boys with stories of their own adolescence, while women can give valuable insights into how girls think.

Most boys are likely to experiment with forbidden substances at some point; if you're lucky, it will just be alcohol and cigarettes; if you're less fortunate, it may involve harder drugs. Parents can reduce the allure of alcohol and teach teenage boys to approach drinking responsibly by allowing them moderate amounts of alcohol in the home – for example, with a weekend meal.

The Institute for the Study of Drug Dependence reports that by the age of fourteen one in three teenagers have tried drugs.[3] Since the maturation of the brain is not complete until late teens or early twenties, prolonged use of drugs in adolescence can be more damaging than in adulthood, and can increase the likelihood of later addiction[4] or depression. The hope is that boys who choose to experiment with drugs move on from them fairly quickly.

Adults can help boys by:
– making it clear they do not condone drugs
– regularly talking about the issues
– keeping abreast of information about drugs
– staying in touch with other adults

When talking to boys about drugs, avoid giving lectures or

making judgments, as this will switch them off. A two-way discussion is more useful, seeking their views and telling them yours. To teenagers, adults warning them off drugs can seem either hypocritical, if the adults have taken drugs themselves, or ignorant, if the adults have had no experience of drugs. Be prepared to acknowledge this, and explain the facts and reasons for your current views. Do not pretend to know anything you don't; rather, ask boys to tell you what they know, and suggest both of you seek further information on the subject.

## Moving towards manhood

The late teens can be a confusing time for young men who, not yet emotionally mature and for the most part still dependent on their parents, nonetheless want to be treated like adults and to take part in the areas of life available to adults.

It is particularly important at this age to listen to boys' views and to seek their opinions in order to demonstrate they are being taken seriously. At the end of a parents' session on boys, a mother approached me for advice. She had four children and felt that her seventeen-year-old son was persistently undermining her authority by being critical of the boundaries she set the younger children. What could she do to stop him undermining her? On discussing it further, it seemed that the seventeen-year-old saw himself as a young adult and wanted his opinions heard, while his mother viewed him as a child who should defer to his parents. I suggested that she acknowledge that he was now a young adult in the household and ask for his support with the three younger children. The parents could explain their principles and thought processes to him and ask him to explain his. If the conversation went well, they would not only enrol their son into the project of raising the family, but also get some interesting feedback on their parenting style thus far.

When adults do not acknowledge a boy's emerging manhood, he may feel obliged to fight for recognition. If the adult perceives this as a threat to his or her authority and attempts to keep the boy in his place, an unhealthy competition emerges between them, resulting in confrontation and argument; sometimes this gets physical. The young stag is instinctively challenging the old stag for his place in the herd. Adults can avoid these head-on collisions by adopting a non-confrontational approach.

Instead of:   'If you want to be treated like an adult, you need to behave like one!'

say:   *'Yes, it is time you were treated like an adult. Maybe we should discuss what that entails.'*

It is right to treat boys in their late teens as young men. However, they still need boundaries to provide a safe structure in which they can grapple with their newfound freedoms. These might include being in at a reasonable hour – especially if they have to be at school, work or college the following day – and setting aside sufficient time for study and for sleep. The reasoning behind boundaries needs to be explained and there should be some room for negotiation. However, there will still be some boundaries beyond which you are not yet prepared to go.

*'Please don't take this personally. I'm not saying I don't trust **you** to have an unsupervised party. What I'm saying is, I don't trust **sixteen-year-olds** to have an unsupervised party. However good your intentions, if some of your friends drink too much and get out of hand, you can't guarantee how they will behave. If you want a party you can have one, as long as you understand that an adult will be on hand.'*

Being treated like an adult has to be two-way: it includes being expected to contribute in some of the ways an adult does. Once boys are fully-grown, they can be tremendously helpful in the home and in the community. Asking them to contribute gives them a sense of responsibility and self-worth. Make sure they know that their input is appreciated.

Teenage boys also need to learn independence. So, instead of relying on adults for lifts, for example, boys can be encouraged to use public transport or a bicycle. Part of independence is knowing how to handle money. They can learn this by earning some money of their own and being expected to use it to pay for clothing and leisure activities. This is a good time for boys to learn from their mistakes. Better for a boy to spend all his money and be broke for a month or so whilst he is a teenager than to have to learn this lesson later in life with bills to pay. Firmness is the watchword here: refusing to give a boy an advance or getting him to pay for a phone bill may initially seem harsh (to him if not to you!), but these disciplines will be invaluable to him as preparation for independent living. Boys who go out to work or get a maintenance grant for college while living at home should be asked to contribute something towards their upkeep. Enabling them to pay their way will give them self-respect. Make sure they are told what a difference their contribution makes.

Clear boundaries and firm discipline throughout boyhood provide a strong foundation for the teenage years. If the boy and the adults around him are emotionally literate (see Chapter 5), they will probably be able to navigate their way through this time without too much grief. For some boys and their parents, however, these years can be difficult. Sometimes it gets so bad that parents, at the end of their tether, tell a boy to move out. This usually happens when emotions are running high, and can be provoked by an underlying situation, such as a boy feeling usurped by a step-parent, or a single mother feeling bullied by her now-grown son. Telling a boy to move out in the heat of an angry exchange may make matters worse and exacerbate any feelings of mistrust or betrayal he already has.

A boy needs to live in a place that provides him with the support he requires until he is sufficiently mature to leave home. To get this support he may occasionally need to move from one home to another, particularly if his parents are separated: some boys want to be with their mother when they are younger, but feel the need to be with their father as they grow older; sometimes confrontation with a parent provokes a move. If a boy needs to move from one parent to another, or to spend time away from his parents, this should be done after reflection, discussion and planning, with a trial period and a time to review the situation.

Everybody matures gradually over his or her lifetime; many of us will remember at eighteen, 21 or 25 thinking, 'I am an adult, but I don't feel like one'. The advent of an eighteenth birthday does not mean a boy will transform into a responsible adult overnight. As he grows up he will mature in some areas faster than others, and will seem mature in some situations but not others. In her book *The Myth of Maturity*, Teri Apter warns us not to expect or assume maturity too early, and flags the need for emotional support of young people between sixteen and 25. Even the boys who seem most able to handle themselves may need more emotional support than they appear to, and may find it difficult to ask for help. During this time, young men need adults, particularly men, to be available to them as they embark on the tricky voyage to manhood.

# Boundaries and Discipline

## Ensure boys know what the boundaries are
- Don't have too many
- Keep them simple
- Adjust them with age

## Apply rules fairly and consistently
- Be consistent
- Ensure boundaries are applied to girls as well as boys
- Give boys take-up time
- Make it clear you do not hold a grudge

## Use positive language to reinforce boundaries
- Speak calmly, avoid shouting
- Instead of asking questions or dwelling on the misdemeanour, remind boys of the boundary
- Acknowledge boys when they do things right

## Keep communication channels open
- Make it easy for boys to tell the truth
- Ask boys for their opinions and listen to their point of view
- Give boys up-to-date factual information about sex and drugs
- Talk with boys before making important decisions about their life

## Sanctions should be:
- appropriate to the misdemeanour
- appropriate to a boy's maturity
- limited in time

NOTEBOOK

Do boys have clear guidelines about what they can and can't do?

Are there any rules that boys might think are applied inconsistently or unfairly?

How can you make sure boys get more attention for what they do right?

What can you do to keep communication channels open?

Devise suitable sanctions for situations where boys overstep boundaries.
Is each sanction fair, limited in time and workable?

*Misdemeanour*                    *Sanction*

## Chapter 4

# Allowing Boys to Be Their Best

*If children live with encouragement, they learn to be confident; if children live with praise, they learn to appreciate; if children live with approval, they learn to like themselves.*

Dorothy L. Nolte

The way adults treat boys can make a huge difference to how they feel about themselves. Boys who feel good about themselves are likely to be happy and confident and to lead more contented, healthy and successful lives.

The *Leading Lads* survey[1] asked 1,344 boys a range of questions to determine their level of self-esteem, what may have influenced this, and what effect it had. Of the boys surveyed 334 had high self-esteem – they were called 'Can-do' boys; 167 had low self-esteem – they were called 'Low Can-do' boys.

'Can-do' boys talked of parents who:

- are loving
- are very helpful
- listen to my problems and views
- like me to make my own decisions
- get my respect
  offer guidance about life
- lay down the right rules
- treat everyone in the family equally

'Low Can-do' boys were more likely to say their parents did not often do things listed above and were likely to do some of things listed below:

— try to control everything I do
— treat me like a baby
— take no notice of me
— argue with me daily or weekly

Other differences between the two groups identified in the survey were:

4% of 'Can-do' boys were anti-school
*43% of 'Low Can-do' boys were anti-school*

2% of 'Can-do' boys suffered from depression
*31% of 'Low Can-do' boys suffered from depression*

14% of 'Can-do' boys had been in trouble with the police
*37% of 'Low Can-do' boys had been in trouble with the police*

*69% of 'Low Can-do' boys were anti-school and/or suffered from depression and/or had been in trouble with the police*

*11% of 'Low Can-do' boys were in all three of these categories (unlike any of the 'Can-do' boys)*

The survey showed that boys with low self-esteem are far more likely to have problems. The rest of this chapter shows how to encourage a healthy sense of self-worth in boys through our day-to-day communication with them.

**To nurture boys' self-esteem:**

- Recognise the best in every boy
- Express expectations positively
- Give boys a positive self-image

### Recognise the best in every boy

When my son was small, my husband had a stressful job with a long journey to and from work. On arriving home he wanted to unwind with a cup of tea and tell me about his day. Our three-year-old was having none of this: he had not seen his dad all day and wanted his attention. Each evening he became very demanding – if he could not get his father's attention himself, he would make sure his father did not get mine. My husband was not pleased at the way our son seemed to be turning out and was stern with him when he displayed this demanding behaviour.

One day, apparently out of the blue, my son said, 'Daddy doesn't like me'. I was horrified, since of course I knew his daddy loved him very much. That evening I told my husband, who was equally appalled. He went to our son and said, 'How's my treasure boy?' The boy's face lit up and he snuggled up with his father. It was a simple thing, but it changed their relationship: our son, realising he was liked and accepted, stopped his demanding behaviour, and his father, understanding his part in the dynamic, started enjoying the boy for who he was, rather than being annoyed with the way he behaved.

Boys pick up on whether they are liked and will respond accordingly. The cues boys pick up from their parents and other adults can have a significant effect on their self-esteem: if a boy feels liked, he will believe himself likeable; if he feels loved, he will believe himself lovable. This sense of self in turn affects his behaviour: a boy who feels good about himself usually behaves well; a boy who feels bad about himself often behaves badly.

Labelling can start early: a baby who sleeps through the night is 'good'; a baby who doesn't is 'difficult'; a boy who cries easily is 'soft'; a boy who likes fighting is 'aggressive'. Whilst it is useful to be able to describe someone's characteristics and for them to know their qualities, these descriptions too often become labels, making it difficult to see the person beneath.

Most characteristics have both a positive and a negative side: someone who is outspoken tends to speak the truth, but can be insensitive to others' feelings; someone who is tolerant can be generous towards others' faults, but might be taken advantage of. Boys skateboarding in urban areas can be seen as unsociable and dangerous, or as skilful and brave.

Finding the positive aspects of boys' characteristics allows you to see them and their behaviour in a positive light. Behind many an apparently negative characteristic is a positive characteristic waiting to be drawn out. When an adult recognises and addresses these qualities in a boy, he will feel understood and able to live up to them.

*Stewart was a confident boy. He knew his own worth, said what he thought, and considered adults his equals. He was popular with his peers, but many adults found him loud, cocky and unco-operative.*

*When the youth club arranged a cross-channel sail-training voyage, Stewart was the first to sign up and, encouraged by his grandmother, raised all the money for his place himself. His father, however, had reservations: Stewart's behaviour had ruined holidays for others before. His father was not the only one with qualms: a parent expressed fears that Stewart's attitude would put the rest of the crew in danger. The youth worker reassured her that the voyage would be safe, but privately wondered how she would manage a week with Stewart without being tempted to throw him overboard!*

*Stewart's grandmother, however, was convinced that the trip would be the making of him. She was right.*

*As they crossed the channel in a strong wind with a following sea, most of the crew succumbed to seasickness. It was Stewart who cheered everyone up with jokes and songs during the crossing, and continued to lead singsongs throughout the week; it was Stewart who initiated the banter around the table at mealtimes; it was Stewart who organised card games when his watch was off-duty; it was Stewart who prepared salad for eighteen without help or guidance; it was Stewart who gave the vote of thanks to the adults at the end of the trip.*

*Stewart's loud voice, quick wit and tireless energy became a contribution on the boat; despite being one of the youngest on board, he was a leader and took charge of group morale. When the youth worker told him what a star he had been, he made a request: 'Will you tell my dad that?'*

*A year later, when he was choosing his study options, he told the youth worker that he was taking catering since he planned to work on cruise liners as a chef.*

---

If you want to build a boy's **character** focus on his positive **characteri**stics.

---

There are some characteristics that are harder to see in a positive light than others, but often these are the ones most worth exploring. A boy who is rude to an adult might be *courageous* to have spoken out; a boy who gets into fights might have a keen *sense of justice*; a boy who is devious may be *clever*; a boy who lies may be *imaginative* or have a strong *survival instinct*. This wider, more generous, interpretation does not, of course, condone bad behaviour.

---

Any **characteristic** or **personality** can be accepted. Certain *behaviours* need to be limited.

---

Make it clear it is the *behaviour* you find unacceptable, not the boy.

| | |
|---|---|
| Instead of: | 'How dare you be so insolent! ' |
| say: | *'The way you said that was very rude.'* |
| | |
| Instead of: | 'You're nothing but a bully. You should be ashamed of yourself! |
| say: | *'I like you Stephen, but I don't like the way you treat your friends.'* |

Instead of: 'That's a pack of lies. I can't trust anything you say! '

say: *'I want to trust you, so I need you to tell me the truth.'*

Looking for a positive *motive* in a boy's behaviour provides the key to understanding how to *motivate* him. A boy who does not like being told what to do probably wants some control over his life; giving him some decision-making power might make him more co-operative. A boy who doesn't want to try new experiences may be afraid of failure; pointing out what he is good at may give him the confidence to try new things. A boy who boasts a lot might want reassurance that he is good enough; some unsolicited words of praise might provide that reassurance.

Most people find attention-seeking behaviour very irritating and often respond by trying to ignore it. Sometimes this works; at other times it just makes it worse. It is worth considering why the boy is behaving like that – in some cases he may actually need some attention! But how can he be given the attention he needs without encouraging further irritating behaviour? The trick is to make a point of giving the boy attention *before* he starts demanding it.

---

Attention seekers need attention.
Give it to them before they ask for it.

---

Whilst attention seeking is annoying, it does have a positive side. At some level, *the child is aware of his needs* and is seeking to have these fulfilled. How much more dangerous is the situation where a boy is unaware of his need for attention, does not seek it, and becomes withdrawn or depressed?

To a boy who is jealous of his little sister:
*'Your sister needs a feed now, then she'll sleep. As soon as I've fed her we can snuggle up and have a story.'*

To the boy who is prone to boasting:
*'Wow, this model has so much detail. You've certainly got a lot of skill – I'm impressed!'*

As he realises he can have your attention when he needs it, the boy will seek it less, and in less annoying ways. By drip-feeding him attention, you wean him off attention-seeking behaviour.

If a boy seems to be operating below his potential, it is easy to dwell on what he is *not* doing rather than on the potential you see. The result is self-fulfilling: a boy who is told he is lazy switches off and does nothing; a boy who is told he is clumsy becomes self-conscious and uncomfortable in his body. Hold up a picture of the boy at his best, then subtly invite him to live up to it.

To a boy with an artistic ability he rarely uses:

*'Your dad loved the last card you made for him. Why don't you make one for his birthday next week?'*
or
*'We need some posters to advertise the event. Will you design one for us?'*

To a boy with a mechanical bent:
*'I can't get anyone to mend this. Would you have a look at it for me?'*

If you demonstrate your confidence in them, boys will live up to it.

To a boy who appears not to be trying at school say:
*'I think you could do very well in this subject.'*

To a boy who is in the habit of getting ready at the last minute say:
*'I know you like to be on time, so why don't you get your things ready five minutes before you need to leave.'*

To boys who are arguing say:
*'I'm sure you can work out a sensible solution to this – come and tell me when you have.'*

*Chris had had a troubled childhood. When he moved into the neighbourhood, aged eight, he used to pick fights with the other boys. By the time he was nine he had such a bad reputation that most parents would not allow him in their homes and many told their children not to play with him.*

*There was one family where he was welcome to play. The mother could see that Chris was a good soul beneath his troubled exterior, and her son enjoyed playing with him. At their house Chris was co-operative and polite.*

*One day she was watching the boys playing with some neighbours, when suddenly Chris punched one of the others.*

*'Hey, Chris, I saw you hit Jack. What was going on there?'*

*Chris explained that a voice in his head had told him to do it, and that was what happened sometimes.*

*'Do you know something,' she said. 'You probably have another voice that talks to you as well, but you need to listen very carefully to hear it. It's like there's a little devil on one of your shoulders whispering things like, 'Hit Jack!' and there's a little angel on the other one whispering, 'No, don't do it!' The more you listen out for the angel, the louder that voice will become.'*

*Chris was taken by the idea and told her that he had a soft toy that was a devil. He insisted on going to get it, and it turned out to be his Manchester United mascot, which he called Biff.*

*A week or so later the boys were play fighting in the garden when Chris started to get out of hand. Jack turned to him and said, 'Don't take this personally,' and threw a punch over Chris's shoulder. 'There, that's sorted Biff out,' Jack explained, and they all carried on with their game.*

### *Express expectations positively*

If you have high expectations of boys and make it clear what these are, they are most likely to reach them. This is true as long as the boy sees the expectations as realistic; if he doesn't, they can have the opposite effect. For example, he understands that you expect him to do as well as his older sister, but sees this as an impossible task. Instead of trying and failing, he may decide not to play the game at all.

Sometimes children hear in our words expectations that we may be unaware of. The warning 'Get down off that wall – you might fall!' can result in a confident, well-balanced child suddenly wobbling and falling off. The child hears his parent's expectation of disaster and fulfils it; he hears the word 'fall' and does what he has been told.

Suppose a small boy is carrying a china bowl across the room. A nervous parent may say, 'Don't drop that bowl, it's breakable!', hoping to ensure that the bowl stays in one piece. But the boy hears the expectation that he will drop the bowl and lets go. He hears the word 'drop' loud and clear – the 'don't' may, or may not, penetrate his brain.

Sometimes I ask groups of teachers to shut their eyes, then ask them what they see when I give them a command. The command 'Don't run in the corridor!' always results in more of them visualising running than walking. Many people's brains find it hard to translate a 'don't' into a 'do'. If it is difficult for adults, how much more difficult must it be for children? Make it easy for them by telling them what you want, rather than what you don't want.

> State expectations positively.

Instead of:  'Don't be late.'

say:  *'Make sure you're back by six.'*

Instead of:  'You always bring mud in on your shoes.'

say:  *'Leave your shoes by the door so the house stays clean.'*

Instead of:  'If you don't work harder, you'll fail your exam.'

say:  *'To get a good grade you need to put some time in every day.'*

Instead of:  'Stop talking.'

say:  *'Let's have quiet.'*

Instead of:  'Don't forget your packed lunch.'

say:  *'Remember your packed lunch.'*

Positive expectations can be a good way to make your values clear.

Instead of:  'I don't expect you to be rude to our neighbours.'

say:  *'I expect everyone in our house to be polite to our neighbours.'*

Instead of:  'You aren't putting enough effort in.'

say:  *'I'd like you to do your best.'*

### *Give boys a positive self-image*

A young person's self-image is heavily influenced by the feedback he or she receives at home, at school and in the community. This section explores how to give a boy feedback that provides a positive, realistic self-image, leaving him secure in his sense of self and able to accurately evaluate his strengths and weaknesses as he moves out into the world.

My stepson started full-time work at sixteen. At seventeen I remember him telling me that he felt his dad, his mum and I had praised him too much as a kid. He explained that at work his bosses were not in the habit of using praise and he badly missed it. He had come to the conclusion that if he had been praised less as a child he would not be in this difficult position.

At the time I was perplexed, since I knew it could not be right to starve a boy of praise throughout his childhood to make sure he was tough enough to weather the world of work. It was only later that I came to understand what the problem might have been: the praise he had received had not given him enough information about himself to know his true strengths and, because adults had always done the evaluating, he had not developed the essential skill of self-evaluation.

Adults often give feedback through praise – 'Good boy!', 'Fantastic!', 'You're a star!' Most boys respond well to this and it makes them feel good. However, it doesn't give them a clear picture of themselves – what it was about him or what he did that made him good, fantastic, or a star. And it may not give a realistic picture: for example, a boy who is constantly told he is clever may expect to be good at everything, then find it difficult to cope when he finds something difficult to understand.

Another way adults give feedback is through criticism – 'You're so lazy!', 'Your room is a pig-sty!', 'I can't trust you'. Most people, including boys, respond badly to these kinds of comments. Not only do they de-motivate, but also they are too broad to give any useful information.

If you want boys to get a clear picture of themselves, give them more specific feedback.

Instead of:   'Good boy.'

say:          *'Thank you for stacking the dishes by the sink'.*

Instead of:   'This is brilliant!'

say:          *'I love this story you've written. It's very exciting.'*

Instead of:   'That's appalling!'

say:          *'Scribbling on your school book makes it look messy.'*

It often works to give feedback with a mixture of description and evaluation:

*'Yuck! You've got food all over your face.'*

*'This sticker collection is great! I like the way you've put each kind on a different page.'*

If you want a boy to learn to self-evaluate, then he sometimes needs to hear descriptions without evaluation and so have the opportunity to assess the situation for himself.

*'You got every answer right.'*
[I understand this topic well.]

*'The lawn looks much neater now.'*
[I'm good with the mower.]

*'Your room has clothes all over the floor.'*
[I'd better tidy up.]

*'I gave you money and didn't get any change.'*
[Whoops, I forgot.]

---

Describe behaviour rather than evaluate it.

---

If the boy does not feel judged, he is more likely to do what needs to be done.

Instead of:  'Stop that, you horrible boy!'

say:  *'Stop that – it hurts when you pull people's hair.'*

It helps to describe without evaluating when there may be a discrepancy between the opinions of the adult and the boy. Suppose a boy has drawn a picture that is good for his age and ability, but does not satisfy him because it falls short of the photographic standard he had in his mind. The well-meaning comment, 'That's brilliant!' provokes the response,

'No it's not, it's rubbish!', and the boy crumples up the picture and throws it on the floor. He was already hurting because the picture did not come up to his own high standards; the adult's inaccurate evaluation merely served to rub salt into the wound. Describing the picture might have proved more helpful to the boy:

*'It's very colourful.'*
*'I like the way the yellow blends into the green here.'*
*'This figure has a real sense of movement.'*

He is unlikely to disagree with these observations, and they may allow him to see the picture in a different light.

You can also get a negative reaction to evaluative praise from someone with a poor self-image. For example, if a boy has decided he is 'thick', then an adult telling him he is 'clever', or even 'good at maths', may just provoke an argument. Teachers have told me of cases where saying 'Good boy' can guarantee half an hour of dreadful behaviour. Perhaps the boy is saying to the adult, 'You've made a mistake, I know I'm a bad boy – let me show you.' Or perhaps he is saying, 'So you like me when I'm good. Will you still like me when I'm bad?' In these cases boys need to be drip-fed factual evidence of their positive traits until they begin to change their view of themselves.

Describing rather than evaluating can seem awkward at first – partly because we're not used to speaking that way, and partly because we have to stop to see the detail before saying anything. It takes a while to move the focus of attention from the general to the particular; but eventually it becomes natural to give feedback in this way.

Having described what a boy is doing, you can help him build a positive image of himself by putting a label on what has just been described.

*'Your bed is made, your clothes are off the floor and the books are on the shelf. That's what I call a **tidy** bedroom!'*

*'You did all your homework without being reminded. It takes **self-discipline** to do that.'*

*'Thank you for giving up your seat when the visitor came. It's nice to know that **chivalry** is still alive today.'*

*'I know you felt silly falling off your bike. I thought it was **brave** of you to let that lady help you.'*

*'The other boys listen to what you say; you clearly have **leadership** qualities.'*

*'I was disappointed you didn't tell me you'd be home late. But on reflection it's the first time for ages that you've not been on time. That makes you pretty **reliable**.'*

Notice that a positive label can be found even when the behaviour described is apparently negative. Don't worry about using words younger boys may not have come across; most boys enjoy complicated words and it does no harm to extend their vocabulary.

Telling someone else about boys' achievements, or telling boys the good things you have heard from others, can make them feel good about themselves.

*'It's a pleasure to have your son in our house – he's welcome any time.'*

*'Miss Taylor tells me you're very funny in the school play. I'm looking forward to seeing it.'*

*'Grandad said you helped him a lot in the garden yesterday.'*

*'Mrs Gupta told me you took her dog home last week when it got out. She was really grateful.'*

Another way of building a boy's self-image is to remind him of his past successes.

To a boy who is trying to get out of doing chores:

*'I remember when you were eight years old and you decided to cook a meal for the family. I thought you would choose something easy, but you insisted on meat pie and got me to teach you to make pastry!'*

To a boy who is resisting his schoolwork:

*'Remember when you were learning your seven times table? You found it hard for weeks, but you practised and practised anyway. Then all of a sudden it clicked and you've remembered it ever since!'*

Whilst it is very important for boys to know how proud you are of them, they also need to be encouraged to be *proud of themselves*:

Instead of:   'I am proud of you.'

say:        *'You must feel very proud of yourself!'*

Instead of:   'I am very pleased with your grades, they're much better this term.'

say:       *'Your grades are much better this term – I bet you're chuffed!'*

Sometimes, however, all a boy wants to hear is that an adult he respects is proud of him. At these times make sure you tell him!

There are occasions when it can seem hard to find anything positive to describe about a boy's behaviour – he just doesn't seem to be doing anything right! The trick then is to describe the nearest thing to what you want to see. When you do this, an unexpected thing happens – the boy usually moves in the direction you want.

To a boy who doesn't want to go to bed:
*'You are half-way up the stairs.'*
He goes upstairs.

To a boy who is often late:
*'You are five minutes earlier than yesterday.'*
He is less late tomorrow.

To a boy who doesn't like writing:
*'You've written two lines already.'*
He carries on writing.

I said it might initially feel awkward describing instead of evaluating, and it sometimes feels ridiculous describing the nearest a boy gets to doing right. However, most people who try it are amazed at the result. This was what one working mother reported:

*I have a five-year-old boy and getting out of the house in the morning is normally the worst part of my day – he won't eat his breakfast and doesn't want to get ready for school. This morning he was at the table, not eating his breakfast as usual, and I said, 'I can see you looking at your toast.' To my astonishment he picked it up and popped it in his mouth. When he'd finished, he got down from the table and I got him ready and out of the house without any problem. It was the most stress-free morning I've had for weeks!*

Describing what boys are doing right reinforces positive behaviour. So, does describing what they do wrong merely serve to reinforce negative behaviour? It seems likely. To get the behaviour we want from boys – at home, at school and in the community – they must hear those around them noticing the things they do right.

> **Go round catching boys doing things right** [2]

# Allowing Boys to Be Their Best

### Recognise the best in every boy

- Look for the positive aspects of each boy's character
- Any characteristic can be accepted; certain behaviours need to be limited
- Give boys opportunities to fulfil their potential
- Demonstrate your confidence in them

### Express expectations positively

- Make sure your expectations are realistic
- State expectations clearly and positively
- Say what you want rather than what you don't want

### Give boys a positive self-image

- Describe what boys have done and let them self-evaluate
- Give boys positive labels for how they are and what they do
- Tell others what boys have achieved
- Remind boys of past successes
- Acknowledge small steps in the right direction
- Go round catching boys doing things right

NOTEBOOK

Identify some of the characteristics you find difficult in particular boys; then look for a positive side to each of them.

*Difficult characteristic*              *Positive aspect*

Think about the boys you know. Are there any whom you realise you don't like?

If there are, then try to identify something likeable about them (if you can't think of anything, ask their friends and others who know them).

Next time you are with them, look for that likeable quality and see if you can find any more.

Use a diary to note the positive things individual boys do over a period of time.

Think of a recent situation where a boy displayed irritating behaviour. What could you have said to demonstrate confidence in his ability to behave well?

Rephrase the following statements as positive expectations:

*'You can go as long as you don't get into trouble.'*

*'Don't forget to hand your homework in tomorrow.'*

*'I'm not prepared to put up with this mess.'*

Turn the following into descriptive feedback:

*'It's great to have you around.'*

*'You're an excellent footballer.'*

*'The way you eat is disgusting.'*

*'That was very unkind.'*

Choose a positive label to describe the behaviour below:

*'You put your things away without being asked. That was ... '*

*'You volunteered to help even though you hate this job. That shows ... '*

*'You brought Jamie over after you'd hurt him. That was ... of you.'*

Think of good news about boys you could tell others. Whom would you tell? What would you say?

Think of an area a boy is currently having difficulty with. Find a time in the past when he displayed the quality he would need to succeed in that area. What could you say to remind him of his past success?

Identify an area where a boy is not doing what you would like. What does he do that is the nearest thing to the behaviour you want? How could you describe this behaviour to him?

**About Our Boys**

## Chapter 5

# Giving Boys an Emotional Vocabulary

*All boys have feelings. They're often treated as though they
don't. They often act as though they don't.*
                    Kindlon and Thompson, *Raising Cain*

Girls' verbal development is generally faster than boys',
giving them a wider and more emotionally rich vocabulary.
This is partly because boys spend more time in action than
girls and less time communicating, giving them less
opportunity to explore the vocabulary of their feelings.
Girls learn to recognise and name their feelings early on,
and so develop the ability to tell those around them how
they feel. Many boys never learn this skill. Physicality, not
communication, is where they feel more at home, and they
frequently express their emotions in physical ways –
running around, playing a competitive sport, whistling or
singing, or hitting out.

As boys get older, many pick up the message from the
media, their peer group or their family that there are certain
emotions boys are not supposed to have. They may be told
that 'boys don't cry' or to 'be a man', and understand from
this that being upset or frightened is not considered
acceptable for a male.

---

*For boys, anger and upset is the same. If someone
upset them, they say 'sod the upset' and get angry.*
                    Michael, aged 11

---

---

**Using physicality to make a point**

It was the1990s, the Spice Girls were in the music charts and 'girl power' had been discovered. In the playground Alan, aged nine, found himself confronted by three girls in his class pointing their fingers at him and chanting, 'Girl Power! Girl Power! Girl Power!' What could he do to stand his ground? He could think of nothing to say to stop their chanting. Suddenly it came to him; he knew exactly what would make them run. He turned round, dropped his trousers and bent over, showing the girls his two bare buttocks! They screamed and fled. Alan was so pleased by the response he had provoked that he didn't mind being sent to the headteacher's office for having 'mooned' in the playground.

---

When boys are upset or afraid, they may feel ashamed: sometimes the shame is buried deep and the boy gives the impression of being unaffected; sometimes the shame kindles anger which is self-directed and turns inward; sometimes the anger is outwardly expressed through kicking, hitting, shouting, or rudeness. From his observations of men, a boy may conclude that anger is an acceptable male emotion; however, when he expresses it himself he may find that it is unacceptable.

Males tend to be more assertive and also more aggressive than females, and testosterone levels rise after aggressive behaviour. I heard of someone that had undergone a female-to-male sex change who reported experiencing as a man sudden intense anger about small things in a way she had not when a woman. Boys need to be tutored in ways to manage aggression and find appropriate outlets for it. Australian parenting expert Steve Biddulph has coined the term TNT (Testosterone Needing Tuition). He compares it to PMT (Pre-Menstrual Tension) and suggests that, just as a good husband understands his partner's PMT, so the adults in a boy's life need to understand his TNT.[1]

The *Leading Lads* survey of British teenage boys throws some light on how boys deal with their feelings:

*There is a widespread belief among boys that 'if you are dying inside, no-one must know'. When boys describe what they do if they feel very down, we hear of behaviour that is not often recognised as depression. If they pick fights and act in anti-social ways they routinely get into trouble. If they stay in their room and listen to music they are 'doing what other teenagers do'. Some boys withdraw, others become aggressive. Very few talk to someone and say how they feel. This disguises their distress and help is seldom offered. 'I wouldn't talk to a friend about a problem – most boys wouldn't. He's a mate – for having a laugh and that.'[2]*

Though many boys do not give the impression of being sensitive (quite the reverse in some cases), they are just as sensitive as girls and they need to be treated as such. I was in a dentist's waiting room once when a mother ridiculed her son in front of the other patients for not wanting to see the dentist on his own. 'You are such a wuss!' she told him so all could hear. 'You have won trophies for rugby but won't see the dentist on your own!'

I could only imagine how the boy smarted inside at this public humiliation; but outwardly he betrayed no sign of it and when his name was called went in on his own. Perhaps he had just had a lesson in the British 'stiff upper lip'.

---

*When a vocabulary of feelings in young boys is missing in their upbringing, they risk growing up to become men at the mercy of their impulses. They remain unaware of their feelings and inarticulate about them. Until we can apply commonly understood words to things, we can't be fully conscious of them. Every step to a higher level of awareness in relationships requires more sophisticated command of language.*

Eli Newberger, *Bringing up a Boy*

---

The rest of this chapter looks at what we can do to help boys become more emotionally competent.

### To give boys an emotional vocabulary:
- Reflect their feelings back to them
- Model the use of emotional vocabulary
- Describe other people's feelings
- Give boys an opportunity to care

### *Reflect boys' feelings back to them*

A boy learns his first words by being given names for the objects around him. And so it is with emotional vocabulary – emotions need to be given names. Help boys recognise and express how they feel by describing the feelings they seem to be experiencing.

To boys coming in from play:

*'You look as though you've been having an exciting time out there.'*

To a boy who has not been picked for a team:

*'You practised so hard, you must be gutted that you're not in the team.'*

Acknowledging an emotion allows boys to accept it and move on. It does not matter if the boy has not come across a word before; the point is to give him a label for his emotion. A very useful word for boys of all ages is 'frustrated'.

To a boy who screws his drawing into a ball:

*'It's frustrating when a picture doesn't come out exactly as you imagined.'*

Adults often try to help by offering solutions. Acknowledging how boys feel is often more powerful than offering a solution, because it gives them the freedom to find a solution themselves.

*There are lots of children playing in the recreation ground, but Tyrone stands on his own. An adult observes: 'It can be lonely when your friends go and play with someone else.'*

*Looking glum, Tyrone agrees; then he suddenly perks up. 'I think I'll ask Ollie if he wants to play Star Wars,' he says and runs off to the other side of the playground.*

Don't worry if you put the wrong label on the emotion. You will soon be put right.

Adult:    *'You seem really upset about your den being ruined.'*

Boy:    *'I'm not upset, I'm angry! The other boys destroyed it – it took me ages to build.'*

Whilst any feeling can be accepted, certain behaviours must be limited.

*'I can see you're angry with Sheldon, but say it with words not fists!'*

*'I understand that you felt I was unfair to send you to your room, but however you felt, it is not OK to scribble on the walls.'*

*'You seem very upset about this, but you need to talk about it without swearing.'*

A boy's anger or sullenness may be masking deeper emotions, such as humiliation, rejection or fear. These underlying emotions can also be acknowledged.

To a boy who has vandalised property after being banned from a club:

*'You must have been feeling really hurt to want to do that.'*

To a boy who refuses to apologise to a neighbour for breaking a window:

*'It will be scary to go and admit to it, but they will admire you for having been brave enough to tell them.'*

Questions may be helpful to check out what boys are feeling:

*'Are you disappointed that you're not going on the trip?'*

*'Are you missing your friends?'*

*'Does it feel like no one is listening to you?'*

*'Do you feel like you're being controlled?'*

The important thing is to hear their answer, not necessarily to try and fix anything. If boys feel truly heard, then they will begin to trust that it is safe to express what they feel.

Often boys deal with fear, pressure or feelings of inadequacy by avoidance. For example, a boy having difficulty with a subject at school may disengage with it and stop doing homework. Apparent laziness might be masking a feeling of being overwhelmed. Some sensitivity may be needed in working out what is going on.

Instead of:    'You won't get decent grades if you never do any work for your exams!'

say:    *'Are you feeling under pressure because of the exams coming up?'*

A word of warning: having done your best to ensure that boys are able to express their feelings verbally, it is important not to get upset when they do – especially if they are a little clumsy at first.

> Don't take it personally when a boy does express his feelings!

### *Model the use of emotional vocabulary*

Boys learn from example, so it makes things easier if the adults around them model the behaviour they want boys to copy (which might include showing affection openly, not holding a grudge after an argument, admitting one is wrong) and try to avoid doing things they don't want boys to do (which might include swearing or hitting).

Boys are particularly interested in what the men in their lives do, and it is great for boys to see men express the full range of emotions when they are watching sport, listening to music or spending time with friends or family. Expressing emotions does not always entail saying something – instead, it may be a whoop of joy or head in hands with disappointment – but in the long run it is useful for boys to be able to say how they feel, if only to give them a head-start in the complex arena of relationships when they grow up!

Adults can play a vital role in developing boys' emotional vocabulary by saying how they feel themselves – especially men that boys hold in high esteem. It will help boys if the feelings you express are authentic and accurately described.

Do you feel disappointed, sad, upset, let down, exasperated, furious, or hopping mad?

*A teenage boy had been asked to clear away after dinner; it was one of his regular household chores. Some time later his father saw the dishes still on the table and yelled angrily at the boy to get the job done. His son shouted back. The father paused, then said: 'To tell you the truth, I'm not so much angry that you didn't do it, as disappointed that after all this time we still have to remind you to do your job.'*

*The boy cleared up without further comment.*

The adjectives listed below give an idea of the range of feelings we experience.

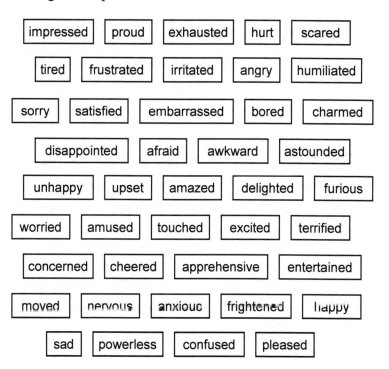

| impressed | proud | exhausted | hurt | scared |
|---|---|---|---|---|
| tired | frustrated | irritated | angry | humiliated |
| sorry | satisfied | embarrassed | bored | charmed |
| disappointed | afraid | awkward | astounded | |
| unhappy | upset | amazed | delighted | furious |
| worried | amused | touched | excited | terrified |
| concerned | cheered | apprehensive | entertained | |
| moved | nervous | anxious | frightened | happy |
| sad | powerless | confused | pleased | |

Some people worry that expressing how they feel will make things worse, and simply create an atmosphere. This certainly can happen, and sometimes it is wisest to say nothing. However, an atmosphere can also be created by what is left *unsaid*; stating what you think and feel can clear the atmosphere and allow everyone to move on.

---

Once you have expressed a negative feeling
– drop it.

---

Recognising how you feel and expressing it whilst it is relatively minor avoids explosions caused by emotions being bottled up for some time.

*'I'm beginning to feel irritated by this level of noise.'*

*'I feel terribly let down when you're unfriendly to visitors.'*

*'Seeing all this mess makes me really angry! I'd like it cleaned up now.'*

It is important that we as adults take responsibility for our own feelings and don't leave the boys feeling blamed for them. Blame causes resentment rather than understanding.

Instead of:  'You make me feel ...'
say:         *'When you do ... I feel ...'*

Instead of:  'You make me furious – you never listen to anything I say!'
say:         *'When you ignore what I say, I feel angry.'*

Instead of:  feeling being taken for granted, or

saying:    'You take me for granted.'

say:       *'When I don't get a thank-you, I feel taken for granted.'*

---

**Nonviolent Communication (NVC)**

In *Nonviolent Communication – A Language for Life*, Marshall Rosenberg suggests a method of communication with others that recognises feelings and needs, and avoids blame.

1. Observe the concrete **actions** that are affecting our/their well-being.

2. Recognise how we/they **feel** in relation to what we are observing.

3. Identify the **needs**, values, desires etc. that are creating our/their feelings.

4. **Request** concrete actions to fulfil these needs.

Instead of:  'How could you be so selfish! You're an hour late and I was out of my mind with worry! If you're going to be so irresponsible, don't expect to be allowed out after dark again.'

say:       *'You came home an hour later than we agreed. I was worried that you might have been in an accident. I need reassurance that you are safe. Next time you expect to be late, will you phone me?'*

---

Telling anecdotes of how you deal with your own feelings gives boys guidance on how to deal with theirs:

*'You know, I dread sorting out the attic – it's such a mess. I've decided that instead of tackling the whole job at once I'll do one bit at a time.'*

*'That's the fifth night running the neighbours' car alarm went off in the night. I was steaming, and nearly went round at 3.00 a.m. to tell them exactly what I thought of them. But I realised I'd probably say something I'd regret, and decided to wait till the morning when I'd had time to calm down and think about what to say.'*

Boys will also learn from you describing other people's feelings:

*'Jack, it really irritates Ben when you sit so close to him. Give him a little space.'*

*'Granny was really upset that you wouldn't do as she asked.'*

While boys will learn from the example of all adults, they are most likely to look to men for role models. If boys see only women express their feelings, they may conclude that this is not something that males should do.

*A father drove his family to his mother-in-law's funeral. Tears were running down his face.*
*'Daddy's crying,' said his son with surprise and curiosity.*
*'Yes, son, I'm very sad today,' said his father.*
*'You loved Nanny, didn't you,' the boy observed.*

When I have suggested to men that boys would benefit from them saying how they feel, some have said that they do not consider themselves particularly sensitive and that they are not the kind of men who 'do emotions'. On being questioned, however, many have acknowledged that they frequently felt angry, and sometimes frustrated or let down. It is exactly these kinds of emotions that boys need to find vocabulary for in order to avoid aggressive behaviour. 'Less sensitive' men would do boys a huge service by showing them responsible ways of expressing anger.

---

*If a role model gives no information about the inner world, then the youngster following that model simply fails to develop an inner world.*

Steve Biddulph

---

Other men explained that showing their emotions was like making a chink in their armour, and that they had spent a good part of their life ensuring their armour was intact. Paradoxically, when a male puts on his 'armour', he increases the likelihood of attack: those around him sense that he is prepared for battle, so ready themselves for it, often deciding that pre-emptive attack is the best form of defence. When a male takes off his armour, others no longer perceive him as a threat, so feel no need to attack. It might be a relief for boys to realise that they do not need armour to survive in the world.

### *Describe other people's feelings*

Boys who find it difficult to express their own feelings might find it easier to relate to the feelings of fictional male characters. Reading, telling stories and discussing books and films with boys can help them recognise and understand feelings. Adults can also talk about the feelings of people on TV, in sport, in the news, or from the neighbourhood or their own childhood.

*'Do you think he felt scared when he did that?'*

*'He must have been devastated when he missed that penalty!'*

Some boys go through stages of showing little empathy to others, and may respond to such conversations in a pretty negative way. Don't get unduly worried about this; exposing them to the idea of how others feel (without lecturing them) will gradually allow them to become more empathetic. Sometimes films or stories can be chosen to help them move down this path:

*When my son was ten, he discovered racist language; he also found out that using it was a wonderful way to wind me up, so my rebuking him only made things worse. I had to find a different strategy. Over a period of months I ordered videos from the library that gave insights into the effects of racism:* Colour Blind, Ghandi *and* To Kill a Mocking Bird. *We watched them as a family and I saw him begin to understand. The racist language stopped.*

*At fourteen he was showing a flair for ice-skating, but when I offered him figure-skating lessons he declined on the grounds that figure skating was 'gay'. By good fortune it was not long before the film* Billy Elliot *was on TV and we watched the story of a miner's son with a talent for ballet. My son's attitude changed and later he accepted the offer of lessons. However, some of the other boys at the rink were horrified to see him wearing figure skates. 'Figure skating is for girls!' they told him.*

*He smiled and reassured them: 'All the best ice-hockey players started off as figure skaters.'*

Boys love heroes and value courage. It is important that this includes *emotional courage*: it might take emotional courage to stand up for what you think is right, to achieve a task against all odds, to keep going when everything looks bleak. You will notice boys exercising their 'courage muscle' from an early age. They need to be taught about the less obvious areas where courage may be needed.

*'It takes courage to stand up for someone who is being picked on.'*

*'Well done on overcoming your embarrassment and asking him to explain how to do it again.'*

*'The more nervous you are about something, the more courage it takes to do it.'*

*'It was brave of you to admit that you did that.'*

*'It was courageous to stick to your principles in that discussion even though your mates were giving you a hard time.'*

145

### *Give boys an opportunity to care*

Boys of every age should be given opportunities to care for others: for their family, for animals, for younger people, the disabled, the old, and the infirm. This allows them to practise taking on responsibility while at the same time developing their softer side.

Asking boys to look after smaller boys gives the younger one a role model of an older boy willing to care for others. Boys make great babysitters and their charges love the fun that boys usually bring to the job.

Getting each child to cook for the family when they reach the age of eleven or twelve allows them to contribute to the household (and get practice for later in life). Raising money for a good cause shows them they can make a difference in the world.

Boys love soft toys as much as girls, and many a teenage boy still keeps his favourite toy animal in his bedroom – sometimes hidden in a private place, sometimes on show for all to see. This is not something to be ridiculed, as it is a welcome sign that his soft side is readily accessible. A teacher in a unit for teenagers with behavioural difficulties used to have a soft toy available during 'circle time' for the youngsters to hold if they were talking about something emotional. The boys liked it so much they would ask for it at other times, and negotiate turns for it with each other.

It can be difficult when boys' sensitivities are not recognised. At youth club recently I heard a ten-year-old girl say she thought a twelve-year-old boy was a wimp because he had cried when he fell over on the football pitch. I didn't want this to pass without comment and said, 'In my experience when someone cries there is usually something to cry about.'

Sometimes boys need to be warned about the kind of attitudes they are likely to come up against:

*'You may get teased if you take your teddy to camp. It's fine by me if you want to take him, but I thought I should warn you.'*

I heard of a ten-year-old boy who took a doll on a weekend residential. He confided in one of his friends, a girl, that he had brought it with him. She told the whole group, and the boy was taunted and laughed at for being a 'sissy'. In these situations adults can give the children a different perspective by the comments they make:

*'Hey, that doll is so cool! Would you mind her being our camp mascot? What's her name?'*

*'Are you guys calling me a sissy? I had a doll till I was 30!'*

*'I don't know about the rest of you, but I've got a stack of soft toys at home. My favourite's a hippo called Blogs. What are your favourites called?'*

*'If it's OK for girls to have dolls, why shouldn't boys have dolls?'*

If the teasing continues, you may need to remind the children of values.

*'We don't have name-calling in this group.'*

## Teenage Angst

The teens can be an emotional time. With hormones racing, boys' sexuality emerges and they become self-conscious of their body and how they look. By the end of their teenage years they are likely to have experienced falling in love, jealousy and rejection.

Boys in love for the first time may wear their heart on their sleeve. When they are rejected, it hurts immensely. In this situation many girls are able to talk to friends, which helps heal the pain. Boys are more likely to deal with their pain privately, and use other strategies to find relief. They may pretend they are unaffected, find respite in physical exercise or sports, blot out the pain with alcohol or drugs, or avoid future hurt by closing down emotions.

> *Is it any wonder that a lot of men have a problem with commitment when so many have had their hearts broken as teenagers?*
>
> Karen Carroll, mother of a 17-year-old boy

Listening to the words of the songs a teenager sings or repeatedly listens to can give an insight into how he might be feeling. Be sensitive if you suspect that something is up. A teenage boy may express his hurt with a foul mood, silence or rudeness. This is not the moment to reprimand him for his behaviour, as it's only likely to make things worse.

Instead of: 'Stop being so foul to your sister!'

say: *'I think Duncan needs a bit of space right now – I'll talk to him about this later. Come with me, Molly: there's something I need to ask you about.'*

Instead of: 'Will you answer when you're spoken to!'
[He does, with some very choice language.]

say: *'You're not your usual self – is anything up?'*

If he does say what's up, he's unlikely to go into much detail, and won't appreciate intrusion into his private life or attempts to sort out his problem. What he might appreciate, though, is some empathy.

Adult: *'How's Megan?'*

Boy: 'We're not going out.'

Adult: *'Oh. I thought you really liked her.'*

Boy: 'She dumped me.'

Adult: *'That must really hurt.'*

Boy: 'It does.'

He may or may not want to talk about it; an empathetic approach indicates that you are there for him if he does.

**Depression**

Everyone feels low from time to time, and young people need to learn how to cope with life's ups and downs. However, a depressed mood that goes on for weeks may become clinical depression, resulting in chemical changes in the brain that cause feelings of hopelessness and lack of motivation. Depression can be brought on by major changes such as moving house or school, divorce, step-parents and bereavement; by worry about bullying, relationships, schoolwork, appearance, sexuality, or money; and by parental or peer pressure.

Symptoms of depression in young people are:
– drop in school performance
– social withdrawal at home or at school
– insomnia or excessive sleep
– lack of concentration / poor memory
– stomach aches / headaches / feeling sick
– apathy / fatigue
– loss or increase in appetite
– drug or alcohol abuse

If you suspect a boy is depressed, seek help. If untreated, clinical depression can last for several months or even years, and is associated with a high risk of suicide.

From around fifteen, teenagers can become fascinated by deep philosophical questions and are often very idealistic. They may share these preoccupations with others or keep them to themselves. Some develop an interest in religion or science; some have deep concerns about global issues; some question orthodox beliefs and practices; some experiment with unconventional belief systems.

Whilst younger children may need black-and-white answers to spiritual questions, teenagers' minds need to question and explore, and they will want to come to their own conclusions. Once a boy is old enough to consider such deep questions, it is healthy for him to do so. If a boy's beliefs are contrary to yours, do not take it personally. Bear in mind that they are likely to change. Denying the validity of his exploration will simply make him exclude you and continue his thought process in private. If you engage with him in the exploration, he may take some account of your views.

This is a time when boys may value discussion. The point is not to come to any conclusions (next month he may think something different), but to help him clarify his ideas by verbalising what he has been thinking. By all means say what you believe, but do not tell him what he ought to think.

*'That's a really important question. Have you come up with any answers yet?'*

*'This is what I think. What do you think?'*

*'In my experience ...'*

*'I used to think ... . Now I think it's more like ...'*

*'For me what's fundamental is ...'*

*Kevin was known as trouble; whenever there was an incident in the neighbourhood, he seemed to have a hand in it. His youth club put on occasional sessions that used games and discussion to explore issues. They were popular and well attended during winter evenings, but numbers dwindled as the evenings grew lighter and warmer. One evening only four teenagers turned up – all boys, one of them Kevin. The youth worker shelved her plan for the session and instead sat and chatted with them about their ambitions, talents and hopes for the future. Kevin said he would leave school after his GCSEs and probably work for his uncle. But his career was not what was concerning him, he explained; right now he spent a lot of time pondering more important questions: Why are we here? What are we here for? What is the meaning of life?*

# Giving Boys an Emotional Vocabulary

## Reflect boys' feelings back to them
- Give names to the emotions boys seem to be feeling
- Name the positive feelings as well as the negative ones
- Acknowledge feelings rather than trying to solve the problem
- Any feeling can be accepted; certain behaviours need to be limited

## Model the use of emotional vocabulary
- Express your own feelings in a responsible way
- Say how you feel yourself
- Tell stories of how you or others dealt with particular feelings
- Describe positive feelings as well as negative
- Once you've expressed a negative feeling, drop it

## Describe other people's feelings
- State how others might be feeling
- Talk about the feelings of other males
- Use music, stories and film to explore feelings
- Give boys an understanding of emotional courage

## Give boys an opportunity to care
- Set up opportunities to help at home and in the community
- Get older boys to help younger boys
- Animals and soft toys can bring out the caring side of boys
- Make it clear that you value boys' sensitivity

NOTEBOOK

With the aim of reflecting their feelings back, what might you say to:

– a boy who says he doesn't like school?
– a boy who hasn't been picked for a team?
– boys who have been fighting?
– boys who have been wrongly accused of causing trouble?

[Say how you think they might feel. Do not try to solve the problem.]

Rephrase these statements to express how you feel about the situation:

– *Look at the state of this room!*
– *Thanks for getting here on time.*
– *You never think about other people!*
– *That was fantastic!*

[Check that you have said what you *feel* about the situation, not what you think about it.]

How could you use the concept of courage to spur a boy to participate in an area where he may feel uncomfortable?

How could you bring out the caring side in boys?

## Chapter 6

# Twelve Ways to
# Avoid Shouting and Nagging

*Adult: How do you react when people shout and nag?*
*Boy: I feel humiliated and resentful, so I switch off.*

When all else fails, adults usually resort to shouting or nagging. Their aim is to obtain co-operation, but nobody likes being nagged or shouted at, and boys often respond by tuning the adult out. They may listen just enough to extricate themselves from trouble, but the rest is a background murmur. It's as though they press the mute button and switch you off.

I came across an interesting, if somewhat unwelcome, concept a few years ago. Researchers had observed that by three years old many children became 'mother-deaf'. The explanation was that mothers typically do the bulk of the care in a child's early years, and as the child becomes more mobile, much of the communication from mother to child centres on what she wants or, more frequently, does not want him to do. As the child develops will and imagination, he learns to tune out his mother's voice to avoid the restrictions of her communication.

Shouting can be extremely useful when there is danger, or to communicate over distance. If it is reserved for these kinds of situations, then boys will learn to hear it and respond positively to it.

There's a saying:

> If you do what you've always done,
> you'll get what you've always got.

So if you want a different result, you need to do things differently. If we define nagging as 'repeatedly asking someone to do something they haven't done previously when asked in that way', then nagging becomes a good candidate for a change of strategy!

Boys hate being lectured at. They usually respond sullenly and, however well the adult states their case, there is no guarantee the message will be taken on board. Dialogue – a two-way conversation that involves listening by both parties – is much more effective, though harder to do. Such conversations are most likely to take place in informal, non-threatening situations, when adult and boy are doing something side by side: car journeys can provide opportunities for dialogue, as can working alongside one another.

Part of the job of an adult is to train the next generation, whether it is to be respectful of their environment, to care for each other, to keep their agreements or to be conscientious in their work. In the training process one thing is sure: boys won't do what you ask them every time and they will need frequent reminding. We have to take care, however, that reminding does not turn into nagging.

This chapter sets out twelve strategies for gaining boys' co-operation without nagging or shouting. Many of the ideas are based on the work of child psychologist Haim Ginott, and authors and parenting experts Adele Faber and Elaine Mazlish. With a little practice these techniques can be extremely effective. The principles underlying them are:

---

Limit what you say.
Keep it positive.

---

### 1. Use a gesture

The best way to limit what you say is to say nothing at all.

*If a boy is too loud, put your finger to your lips.*

*If a boy comes in with dirty trainers, point to them and make a grimace.*

*If someone is sitting on the table, gesture getting off it.*

*If a rule is being broken, point to the notice where that rule is written.*

Making the gesture humorous usually appeals to boys. I met a teacher working in a special unit for teenagers who used to hold her nose when she thought she smelled 'bullshit'. The boys laughed, but knew they had been caught out.

## 2. Say it in a word

In *How to Talk So Men Will Listen,* Marion Woodall highlights the different ways men and women communicate. She suggests that the purpose of communication for women is often to build relationship: hence the habit of using a lot a detail to create context and intimacy. For men, however, the purpose of communication is more often to exchange information; men prefer facts and are irritated by what seems unnecessary detail. This also applies to boys: keep what you say to them short and to the point – an effective way to do this is to use just one or two words.

To a boy whose seatbelt is undone: *'Seatbelt.'*

To a boy who tends to forget his packed lunch: *'Lunchbox.'*

To a boy who has come downstairs after bedtime: *'Bed.'*

Notice that the main word chosen is a noun, not a verb, and it is being used more as a reminder than a command. However, little boys might enjoy being given commands as part of a game – when going for a walk, for example, they could pretend to be a dog ('Heel', 'Sit', 'Stay') or a soldier ('Atten-tion!', 'Quick march!').

People often ask whether these one-word reminders should be followed by 'please'. If you want boys to learn to say 'please', they do need to hear the adults around them setting an example. However, if a respectful tone is used, the word 'please' may not always be needed. The tone of voice often conveys a lot more than the words themselves, so a harsh or abrupt delivery of a command such as 'Quiet please!' can completely negate the respect implied by the word 'please'.

### 3. Give information

Boys learn at a very young age to protect themselves from perceived attack. Being told off by a figure of authority is invariably perceived as an attack, and boys can react by shutting down or aggressively defending themselves. Make it easier for them to hear your message by giving them straightforward information.

| | |
|---|---|
| Instead of: | 'This room is like a pigsty! Come and clear it up right this minute!' |
| say: | *'The clothes on the floor need to be put away.'* |

| | |
|---|---|
| Instead of: | 'Who left this mess in the kitchen?' |
| say: | *'Whoever used the kitchen needs to clean it up.'* |

| | |
|---|---|
| Instead of: | 'I'm sick of having to tell you to do your homework. Don't think you'll be going out with your friends today!' |
| say: | *'As soon as you've finished your homework you can go out and see your friends.'* |

When a boy asks a question, give him a short informative answer.

| | |
|---|---|
| Boy: | 'Where's my jacket?' |
| Instead of: | 'Can't you look after any of your things? Do I have to do everything for you?' |

say:          *'In your room.'*

or:           *'I don't know. Try your room.'*

Some parents find they spend a lot of their time saying 'No', which becomes dispiriting for both them and their children. You can get round that by saying what is possible. The more specific you are, the more likely the boy is to go away satisfied.

Boy:         'Can we go to the park?'

Instead of:   'No.' / 'Not today.' / 'Later.'

say:          *'We are going tomorrow.'*

or:           *'We can go after lunch.'*

Boy:         'Can I have an ice cream?'

Instead of:   'No.' / 'Not today.'

say:          *'We are having ice cream for pudding today.'*

or:           *'Friday is ice cream day.'*

or:           *'If you are happy to pay for it yourself.'*

Boy:         'Can you buy me some new trainers?'

Instead of:   No.' / 'Not today.' / 'Have you any idea how broke I am at the moment?!'

say:          *'I will buy you a pair at the end of the holidays.'*

or:           *'I'm prepared to contribute £25 towards a pair and would like you to pay the rest.'*

### 4. Describe the problem

Boys are natural problem solvers, but are far more interested in finding a solution than dissecting the problem. They get turned off when adults go on about a problem. Simply describing a problem can allow boys to work out for themselves what behaviour is required.

Instead of: 'Late again!'

say: *'This is the second time you've been late this week.'*

Instead of: 'Why haven't you done your homework?'

say: *'That homework is due in tomorrow.'*

Often describing what you see or hear is sufficient.

Instead of: 'Right, that's it! I let you stay up late as a treat and you won't settle down. Don't expect to stay up late again!'

say: *'I can hear talking.'*

Instead of: 'I can't believe the state of this room!'

say: *'There's paper all over the floor.'*

### 5. State how you feel (then drop it)

An adult's anger, frustration or worry is often expressed through shouting or nagging. Boys are likely to respond defensively to this, and some boys' defensiveness sounds aggressive. A boy will hear and understand the adult's feelings better if they are expressed explicitly and without blame.

Instead of:   'You left the place in such a state, we're not going to the film!'

say:   *'When I saw the state of the place, I was upset and disappointed.'*

Instead of:   'What kind of homework do you call this?'

say:   *'I feel really frustrated when I see someone of your ability produce such scruffy work.'*

It is important the emotions described are real; otherwise boys are likely to feel manipulated and may come to distrust expressions of emotion.

Make sure you take ownership of how you feel, rather than blaming the feeling on someone else.

Instead of:   'Your selfishness makes me really angry!'

say:   *'When the phone bill comes in this high, I worry about how we're going to pay it.'*

When there is no blame, the boy does not have to defend himself, so is likely to accept what he hears and learn from it.

Once you have stated how you feel, draw a line under it and move on.

### 6. State positive expectations

When expectations are not being met, it is helpful to restate them in a positive way.

Instead of:  'Look at the state of this room!'

say:        *'I expect you to clean up after yourself.'*

Instead of:  'I can't believe how lazy and ungrateful you lot are!'

say:        *'I expect everyone to help put the equipment away after it has been used.'*

Instead of:  'What do I have to do to get you to come in on time?'

say:        *'When we agree a time, I expect you to honour it.'*

Restating rules will remind boys of your expectations.

Instead of:  'How dare you use language like that!'

say:        *'We have a 'no swearing' rule here.'*

### 7. Point out what needs to be done

Some boys find a large task or a lot of instructions overwhelming. Many respond better if given a single task or instruction, then another one after that is completed. This principle can be used to help boys do their homework.

When things are not right, it is tempting to dwell on the negative, but this is a major turn-off for boys. It is more productive to focus on positive action – what can be done to put things right and what benefit there will be for the boy in doing it. This gives boys direction and an incentive to act.

Instead of:   'Who made this mess?'

say:          *'Let's get this mess cleared up.'*

Instead of:   'You can't leave until this mess is cleared up.'

say:          *'As soon as this mess is cleared up you can go.'*

Instead of:   'Of course you fell off if you rode with no
              hands!'

say:          *'You'll be more stable on your bike if you
              keep your hands on the handlebars.'*

Instead of:   'If you don't work, you'll fail your exams.'

say:          *'If you do your homework, you'll pass your
              exams.'*

### 8. Use humour and playfulness

A good way to avoid nagging and shouting is to be playful and to use humour to lighten the atmosphere. Boys love humour, and, once they are laughing, usually enjoy complying.

---

*Change a mood, not a mind.*
Faber and Mazlish

---

Humour is a personal thing and what works for you will depend on your style of humour, the particular situation and the age and temperament of the boys.

*A small boy is resisting having a bath. The parent inspects his hair and exclaims, 'Luke, I can see some creatures living in your hair! I think you need a bath!', then swoops the giggling boy upstairs.*

*A boy has done something wrong. The adult acts like a zombie and pretends to throttle him.*

*A teenage boy has been sitting out at a barn dance. His godmother approaches him. 'Geoff, if I don't see you on the dance floor, I'm going to ask you to be my partner for the next dance!' He grimaces, decides he'd rather be seen dancing with his cousin than his godmother, and asks his cousin to dance. They have such fun that he is easily persuaded to dance during the rest of the evening.*

*Two teenagers are play fighting and don't stop when asked to. One is bigger and stronger than the other, and has overpowered him. Other boys are watching. The adult says to the smaller boy: 'Hey, why do you always target the weak and vulnerable? I suppose you'll pick on me next!' The boys stop fighting as everyone laughs.*

One family I know has borrowed one of their family rules from *Monty Python*:

*Rule number one is 'No whingeing!'*
*Whenever one of the children starts whingeing, a parent asks, 'What's rule number one?'*
*And the child replies, often with a sheepish grin, 'Rule number one is "No whingeing!"'*

*When they go camping, they ask the children, 'What's rule number one of camping?' With shrieks of laughter the children chorus, 'Don't fart in the tent!'*

---

**Try pressing the rewind button**

Faber and Mazlish[1] suggest giving everyone a second chance when things go wrong by 'rewinding' and replaying the scene in a different way. You can introduce the idea by first using it yourself:

*'That's not what I meant to say; I think I'd better rewind. Right, what I meant to say was ...'*

Later give the boy an opportunity to rewind:

*'It sounds like you might want to rewind. Let's go back to the beginning.'*

Once boys understand the concept, it can be used to defuse quite explosive situations, for example:

A boy comes in late and you confront him. He loses it and swears at you. You say, *'Neither of us did that very well. I think we need to rewind. Why don't you go out, come back in and I'll try again.'*

Later, boys may use the technique themselves.

*'Sorry, I didn't mean to be rude. I'm going to rewind.'*

As well as using 'rewind', try 'cut' and 'take two'.

---

### 9. Break the problem into manageable chunks

Boys are often overwhelmed by the size of a problem – for example, clearing away their toys, tidying their bedroom or doing their homework – and then respond by doing nothing or, when they are older, by filling their time with displacement activities such as texting friends, playing computer games or listening to music. You can help them by asking them to do smaller, clearly defined amounts.

Instead of:   'I said, "Clear the table"!'

say:         *'Please will you put the glasses on the top rack in the dishwasher.'*

Instead of:   'I've asked you to tidy your room and you're just lolling around on the bed! Do I have to do everything in this house?'

say:         *'Start by taking everything off the floor.'*

then:       *'That looks better already. Now put the clean clothes away and the dirty ones in your wash bin.'*

then:       *'Looking good! Just shut each drawer and the job's done.'*

Instead of:   'You moan about there being no food in the house, and then can't be bothered to help me bring the shopping in from the car.'

say:         *'I'd like everyone to bring two carrier bags in from the car please.'*

or:         *'Let's see if we can get all the shopping into the kitchen in three journeys.'*

Instead of:   'Stop making such a meal of it; it's only eight pages!'

say:        *'Have a go at reading three pages.'*

then:      *'That's almost half! Now try three more.'*

then:      *'Two more pages and you've done it.'*

Instead of:   'I can't believe you were chatting to your friends on MSN when you should have been doing your homework!'

say:        *'That's quite a big project you've been asked to do. You probably need to do it one step at a time. How are you getting on with it so far?'*

then:      *'Maybe you should chat to your friends on MSN as a reward after you've done each section. What's the next bit you have to do?'*

and/or:     *'Tell your friends that your wicked parent is making you do your homework, and that you'll be back online in an hour or so.'*

If boys are feeling a bit overwhelmed by the task in hand, they sometimes hear a nag when you don't intend one. If you suspect this, be a little gentler, to make it clear you are on their side.

Instead of:   'Is the room tidy yet?'

say:        *'How are you getting on?'*

or:        *'Do you need any help?'*

Instead of:   'Do you have everything ready for school tomorrow?'

say:      *'Shall I make you hot chocolate while you get everything ready for school?'*

### *10. Put it in writing*

The written word can be a very effective form of communication. It gives the adult time to think about what needs to be said and the boy some space for consideration. Notes can be written on a board, pinned up, left in a message book, handed to a boy, put on his pillow, slid under a door, or duplicated and given out.

A sign by the door:

*Leave dirty trainers outside.*

Before a club outing, a reminder goes up on the board:

*Meet in the car park tomorrow at 9.00 a.m.*
*Bring a packed lunch and a jacket.*

A notice in the park:

*Put litter in the bin. Thanks.*

A note on the bed:

*I am doing the washing tomorrow. Put your dirty clothes in the wash bin before you go to bed. xxx*

A five-a-side game got out of hand at youth club. The next week, the youth worker gave a sheet of paper to everyone who had been playing. It read:

*You are welcome to play 5-a-side in the hall as long as you have a referee with a whistle. A whistle can be borrowed from the club. These are the rules of 5-a-side: ...*

Many boys find it hard to be organised, especially when they are going through growth spurts. As their brains rewire, organisational skills go by the board, so to help them they need support structures such as notice boards, lists and timetables with clear information, prominently displayed.

### 11. Countdown

Counting can inject a sense of urgency or competition into the task in hand; boys often respond well to this, especially if it is done with energy and humour. You can count up from one, or down to zero (as though launching a rocket), speeding up to add excitement or slowing down to help them succeed. With older boys, you can hold one hand up with fingers and thumb outstretched, point to it with the other hand, and then silently bend in the fingers and thumb one at a time.

*'I want this room tidy by the time I count to twenty!'*

*'You said you would come to dinner as soon as that game finished. I'm counting down from ten. Ten... nine...'*

*'I asked for the ball. I'll give you five.'*
*(Hand up and silent count down with thumb and fingers.)*

### 12. Brainstorm the problem

A combination of the above techniques works in many situations, but if there is a recurring or intractable problem, then it is worth taking some time to explore it together and look for possible solutions. Boys like being consulted, and often come up with imaginative solutions to a problem.

Here are some guidelines for brainstorming:

- Choose a time when any emotions have subsided.

- Write down a simple description of the problem.

- Make sure everyone knows the three rules of brainstorming:
  1. Think of as many imaginative solutions as possible.
  2. Every idea is written down.
  3. No comments must be made on ideas until they have all been written down.

- Write down the suggested solutions to the problem; adults can add ideas too.

- Once all the ideas have been written down, assess them together. If anyone disagrees with an idea, cross it out. If everyone agrees with it, tick it. It's fine to add extra ideas or adapt ideas at this stage.

- Talk through the ideas until you agree on a way to solve the problem.

*At twelve years old, Josh was resisting having a bedtime. There were arguments every night. Once in bed it was a long time before he fell asleep. He was grumpy and unco-operative in the morning. Every five or six weeks he got a cold or a cough and stayed off school. Josh wanted to be in charge of his own life and didn't see the point of going to bed if he couldn't sleep. The parents thought the lack of sleep was affecting his mood, his learning and his health.*

*One afternoon parent and son sat down with a pad of paper and brainstormed the problem.*

---

**PROBLEM – JOSH'S BEDTIME**

<u>Ideas</u>

*No bedtime*

*Bedtime in term time, more relaxed in holiday time*

*Watch TV till midnight*

*Stop TV / computer games earlier so brain calms down*

*Listen to music in bed*

*Sleep in and don't go to school*

*Bath before bed to relax*

*Set own alarm clock for morning*

*Back massage if in bed by 9.00 p.m.*

*Be pleasant in mornings, sleep or no sleep*

*Josh in charge of bedtime as long as he doesn't get ill*

---

*Each of these ideas was considered and a plan eventually agreed upon.*

*Josh would be allowed to put himself to bed at a time of his choosing as long as the following conditions were kept:*

- *His homework was done by 8.30 p.m.*
- *His TV and computer were off by 9.30 p.m.*
- *No one else could hear any noise from him after they went to bed.*
- *He got himself up in the morning and went to school without any fuss.*
- *He did not miss school through illness.*

*If any of these conditions were not met, then for the next three days Josh would have to be in his room by 9.00 p.m., with lights out by 9.30.*

*For the rest of the school term the atmosphere changed. There were no arguments about homework or bedtime. Josh got himself up in the morning, and was pleasant to the rest of the family before school. He went to sleep quite late and got grey beneath his eyes, and his parents privately predicted how long it would take him to fall ill. After a couple of weeks Josh developed a cough, but insisted he was fine; then for the next few nights he had a hot bath and put himself to bed early to make sure he did not miss school through illness.*

## What if this doesn't work?

If you don't get co-operation through one approach, try another. For example, you want boys to take their shoes off before coming into the house.

Put it in writing:
*Put a 'Leave shoes here' sign by the door.*

Use a gesture:
*Point to the boy's shoes / point to the sign.*

Say it in a word / phrase:
*'Shoes.'*

Use humour:
*'No smell of socks in here – something's amiss!'*

Give information:
*'There's a shoes off rule for kids in this house.'*

Countdown:
*'Shoes in the porch by the time I count to seven!'*

Describe the problem:
*'There's mud on the floor.'*

State how you feel:
*'I'm really annoyed to see mud on the floor.'*

State expectations:
*'I expect shoes to be taken off at the door.'*

Say what needs to be done:
*'Take your shoes off and clean up this mud.'*

Break down the problem:
*'Everyone pick up three clumps of mud, please, and put them in this carrier bag... Thank you!'*

Whilst it's unlikely you will need to use all these approaches at one time, you will no doubt be given opportunities to practise them all over a period of time! Remember to give boys 'take-up time'. Assume they will do as you say and give them a bit of space to do it.

*I once worked with the staff of a youth drop-in centre that provided information and counselling to young people. They found it was mostly girls who took advantage of the counselling services, but mainly boys that used the facility as a place to hang out.*

*When I asked staff what they found hardest about working with the boys, they said swearing and spitting. They wanted to know how to prevent these unpleasant habits in the centre without getting unduly heavy or banning vulnerable boys from the facility.*

*Simply identifying the problem was a good first step. Each worker found these habits distasteful, but had felt alone in their distaste, not realising that all their colleagues felt the same way. They had believed that providing a safe haven for the boys required them to put up with the boys' unsocial habits. Once the adults realised that the swearing and spitting distressed everyone, they agreed it should be stopped and worked out some simple strategies to do this:*

*Clear rules of expected behaviour would be put up. A swear word could be met with a look, a finger to the lips or the word 'Language'.*

*Workers could express how they felt about it, e.g. 'I was so embarrassed when I showed the visitor round and heard you swearing.' / 'I feel physically sick when you do that: if you need to spit, go to the toilet.'*

*A few months later I dropped in to see how they were doing. Swearing and spitting were no longer issues. The staff had focused on them firmly and consistently, and the boys had responded. Boys were often unaware they had sworn, and an adult just saying 'Language' often provoked the response 'Sorry'.*

# Twelve Ways to Avoid Shouting and Nagging

**Limit what you say.**
**Keep it positive.**

1. **Use a gesture** – Point to the bin.

2. **Say it in a word** – 'Bin.'

3. **Give information** – 'Litter goes in the bin.'

4. **Describe the problem** – 'There are sweet papers on the ground.'

5. **State how you feel (then drop it)** –
'I find it very frustrating to have to remind you to put litter in the bin.'

6. **State positive expectations** – 'I expect everyone to put their litter in the bin.'

7. **Point out what needs to be done** – 'Those sweet papers need to go in the bin.'

8. **Use humour and playfulness** – 'Looks like there's been a tornado round here.'

9. **Break the problem into manageable chunks** –
'Bring me six pieces of litter.'

10. **Put it in writing** – 'Litter in the bin please.'

11. **Countdown** – 'I want the floor clean by the time I count down from 20!'

12. **Brainstorm the problem** –
Define the problem: Litter is not being put in the bin. Write down as many imaginative ideas as possible. Agree on a workable solution.

NOTEBOOK

In what situations do you find yourself most likely to:

– nag boys?

– shout at boys?

What could you do or say to avoid nagging or shouting in those circumstances?

**About Our Boys**

## Chapter 7

# What Men Can Teach Boys

*Masculinity is bestowed. A boy learns who he is and what he's got from a man, or in the company of men, he cannot learn it any other place.*

John Eldredge

Boys learn about manhood from men. From an early age they notice the differences between boys and girls, and between men and women. Although they pick up values and behaviour from all the adults around them, boys will consciously or unconsciously make a point of observing men to find out what maleness entails.

Boys take an interest in men in general, and their fathers in particular. The father is a key role model for boys, as they will learn more from him about what it means to be male than from anyone else. It is natural for children to idolise their fathers at certain periods of their life – this will happen whether or not the father lives with the child. Steve Biddulph suggests that boys tend to focus more on their mother than their father until they are about seven years old; between seven and about fourteen their focus turns to their father; after fourteen they look for male role models outside their immediate family. While a boy wants his mother and father to be there for him throughout his life, each parent should be prepared to step forward or back at certain times to meet his need for space or a particular sort of attention at that time.

Fatherhood brings with it joys, responsibility and sometimes an unexpected emotional journey. It starts with the miracle of birth and intense feelings for the tiny thing that is yours to protect. Shock may follow when the responsibility of what you have taken on sinks in. A few weeks of interrupted sleep and exhaustion sets in. As the mother follows her biological urge to focus completely on her baby, the father may begin to feel ignored or taken for granted. This can be compounded if she then goes off sex for a while. At this point a father might wonder what he's got himself into: the woman he adored devoted her time and attention to him before; now not only does the baby have all her time and attention, but it also has first call on her body!

Forgive me for focusing on the negative, but what I am describing is the first hurdle of parenthood. It is a hurdle that many overcome, but for some couples the advent of a child, however loved, is the point at which the first crack in the relationship occurs. At the time it seems as though the difficulties encountered are to do with the couple; but if the father moves on to a new partner and they decide to have children, the same thing is likely to happen all over again.

To overcome this and other hurdles, fathers need a network of friends and relatives who understand the process of parenting and can provide them with emotional support while they support their family.

Fathers cannot single-handedly provide everything a boy needs from men; boys need access to a range of male role models, so they can follow their own interests and learn a variety of skills and ways of being. These men will often fall naturally into a boy's life: a neighbour, uncle, grandfather, or friend of the family; a teacher, club leader or coach. Often the relationship flourishes without encouragement; sometimes a parent needs to ask a particular man to spend some time with the boy.

A stepfather can contribute a lot to a boy, but there is also potential for conflict. Competition is inevitable between a boy and any partner his mother has. However well they get on, two things will be clear to the boy – this man is not his father, and he is sleeping with his mother. The upset this causes the boy can result in rudeness and bad behaviour. The competition will lessen if a partner or step-parent recognises that the relationship between the parent and children comes first, and that he must endorse that prior relationship. Then, instead of the two males competing for the mother's love and attention, the boy feels that his place in her heart is secure and therefore he can include this man in his life. It is not uncommon for a new partner to think that the mother is being too soft on her son, and to try to help improve discipline. Sadly, this often makes things worse; it is much better for the parent to continue to be responsible for laying down the rules – the new partner's job is to be her trusted lieutenant.

### How men can teach boys what they need to know
- Spend time with boys
- Be a role model
- Guide them into manhood

## *Spend time with boys*

Boys with a man in their life who spends time with them, does activities with them, listens to their problems and gives them guidance are most likely to have high self-esteem and a positive outlook toward school.[1]

Men can involve boys in their own interests and activities, and introduce them to the things they themselves used to like to do as boys. A lot of boys just like hanging out with men, watching and helping. When a man shares what he loves with a boy – music, sport, wildlife, fishing, computers, reading – he is giving part of himself to that boy. Sport can provide a great common interest and strong bond between males. If you don't like the same sports as the boy, if one of you is sporty and the other is not, or you don't share each other's interests, then look for something new you can do together.

Every child wants dad all to him- or herself at times, without having to share him with anyone else. This may involve snuggling up for a story, having a kick around or watching a film together. There are times when boys and men need to be together doing things in their way, without any females in their midst. Women should take a step back at these times and enjoy the opportunities it gives them to spend time on their own, with their daughters or with other women.

Boys love it when men notice them – they feel seen. It doesn't have to be much, just a comment in passing. I often say 'Hi' to the kids in our village, which they seem to like.

But when my husband says something to the boys – often some crack about football – there is a greater response: they light up, rise to his challenge and reply with a bit of banter. They are responding to his maleness. The same happens at the youth club when men help out: both the boys and the girls love the special kind of energy they bring.

If you get to know local boys, just by passing the time of day or making a joke with them, you will become part of their world – someone they value and respect. The pay-off comes when they move into a mischievous or crazy stage of their lives. A word from you and they will probably listen.

In his book *Wild at Heart*,[2] John Eldredge tells of a time he took his sons Sam and Blaine rock climbing. Sam got stuck at an overhang and his dad offered to lower him down on the rope:

*'No,' he said, 'I want to do this.' I understood. There comes a time when we simply have to face the challenges in our lives and stop backing down. So I helped him over the overhang with a bit of a boost, and on he went with greater speed and confidence... As Sam ascended I was offering words of advice and exhortation. He came to another challenging spot, but this time sailed right over it. A few more moves and he would be at the top. 'Way to go, Sam. You're a wild man.' He finished the climb, and as he walked down from the back side I began to get Blaine clipped in. Ten or fifteen minutes passed, and the story was forgotten to me. But not to Sam. While I was coaching his brother up the rock, Sam sort of sidled up to me and in a quiet voice*

*asked, 'Dad, do you really think I was a wild man up there?'*
*Miss that moment and you'll miss a boy's heart forever. It's*
*not a question – it's the question, the one every boy and*
*man is longing to ask. Do I have what it takes? Am I*
*powerful? Until a man knows he is a man he will forever be*
*trying to prove he is one, while at the same time shrink*
*from anything that might reveal he is not. Most men live*
*their lives haunted by the question, crippled by the answer*
*they have been given.*

### Be a role model

Whatever men do provides a role model for boys. The way
they spend their time, tell jokes, talk about themselves and
other people; their attitude to work, to women, to alcohol, to
sex; all these things and others will be acutely observed and
absorbed by boys.

There are some things boys can only learn from being in the
company of men. Male humour for example – what kind of
humour can be used to entertain everyone, and which is
better kept from female ears. They can learn about swearing
– not just whether to swear, but how to swear, and when
and where not to.

Boys can learn about competition from men, about
commitment and teamwork, about being a good winner and
a good loser. Boys can learn about justice, about
authenticity, about self-control. Men have a great way of
being simple, direct and telling it how it is. This usually
works well with boys. Sometimes men get angry with boys,
sometimes very angry, and this can be just what's needed –

the boys get in line and everyone moves on. At other times men can lose control and go over the top; then boys endure rather than learn from the man's anger. If the anger is too powerful for the relationship or situation, the boy may withdraw and need a lot of drawing out in the future. In some boys that anger will trigger a violent reaction.

Men can teach boys about respecting women. Boys pick up on the affection and respect between their parents, and on teamwork between men and women working together. If a boy's parents are separated, however painfully, the boy can learn from hearing his father talk respectfully to and about his mother. Men can help boys recognise when joking about sex or girls is just a laugh and when it's disrespectful.

Men can teach boys to love learning and knowledge. Every man I know, whether he liked school or not, has certain topics he knows a huge amount about, and a curiosity to learn about the world. Men can also teach boys to enjoy reading. There is a worrying phenomenon in schools at the moment – at every age, boys on average perform 10% less well than girls. Reading is one area of concern. If boys see only females reading and are read to only by their mother and women teachers, they may conclude that reading is not a male activity. To get the message that reading is something males do, they need to see men reading too. It doesn't have to be anything you wouldn't do already; just reading a newspaper or magazine when boys are around and getting a magazine or comic for them might be all that's needed.

More important than reading, boys need to hear men telling stories, stories about anything and everything, but also *their* stories – as man and boy. They don't need lectures ('You don't know how lucky you are – when I was a boy…'); they need to hear it how it is: the pleasure, the pain, the successes and failures and, more than anything, the adventures.

Another thing boys benefit from knowing is that being a man does not mean being Superman. Superman is something boys play at when they are young. A man should be content to be himself, with his unique set of characteristics, strengths and weaknesses.

When researching my book for teachers, I noticed that a lot of boys had a problem asking for help at school. They didn't want to risk the humiliation of being shown up in front of their friends. Actually, a lot of men don't seem to like asking for help either – the classic scenario is when a man and woman are out in the car and can't find the way: the man resists asking for directions, then when he finally concedes they need help gets the woman to ask someone.

When exploring this with teachers, I've asked the men whether they found it hard to ask for help and, if they did, why this might be. Quite a lot said they did, and one explained that he felt he was supposed to know everything and be able to do everything; therefore asking for help was an admission of failure. His dad had seemed capable and knowledgeable, omniscient in fact; so as far as he was concerned that was how a man should be.

Boys need to know it is OK both to ask for help and to say 'I don't know'. They will find this easiest if they see men doing it, especially if this is their father or principal role model.

Boys pick up what it is to be a man almost by osmosis, just by being around men. In this process they learn many things. There are also some things men learn, or remember, from being with boys – to stay connected with who they are, to have fun, to tell the truth and to maintain a sense of humour.

A man continues to be a role model to a boy even when he dies. The boy holds his own memories of that man, and adults can build up a fuller picture by talking about him to the boy.

*Winston's Wish is a charity that runs residential weekends for bereaved children, to help them come to terms with their loss. They encourage children to bring a photo of him- or herself with the person they have lost. One eight-year-old boy selected a photo of his father on his own – standing on a podium having won a motor racing event. His mother asked him what had made him decide on that photo and what the other boys in his group might think of his dad. That he was a winner, the boy said, that he was great fun, took risks and all his team-mates liked racing with him. She asked him what advice his dad would give him about going to Camp Winstons. 'Oh, he'd say, "Have a go, make friends, have fun, Mum's not far away".'*

*Despite not having slept alone since his father's death, the boy threw himself wholeheartedly into the weekend, made lots of friends and enjoyed the sleepover.*

### Guide them into manhood

In many tribal cultures, boys go through an initiation process that marks their movement into manhood. Typically men of the tribe take the initiates away from their mothers to spend time in an unfamiliar place and partake in a series of experiences that challenge the boys on a physical, emotional and spiritual level. They leave as boys and return as young men. The whole community is aware of this change, and while some may mourn the loss of their boy, all celebrate the return of the young men.

In our culture there is no clear moment when boys are acknowledged as young men, and no celebration of the change, since young men are often regarded as a potential problem. In the absence of ritual initiation, perhaps boys use getting drunk, having sex, or driving fast as methods of initiating themselves. There are physical signs that a boy is moving toward manhood: he grows taller than his mother; his voice breaks; he starts to shave. When these things happen, it is time for men to step forward and guide the boy through the next part of his journey.

This may be done formally or informally, by one man or several. It might entail hanging out together, going on a journey, having an adventure or working alongside one another. It is not a time to compete with young men or put them in their place; it is a time to give them new experiences, offer them challenges and welcome them into the tribe of men.

The key element is sharing, the sense of being part of something with adult men. Young men need to be given the opportunity to take the lead in a shared task. It can be something very simple: to fix something, plan an activity, work out a route for a journey, cook a meal, put some flat-pack furniture together. The important thing is that they are given the trust and respect to share an activity as equals, where their leadership is respected by someone they respect and long to be respected by. The milestones on the journey from boy to man are many and varied, and such simple steps as these guide boys towards their next milestone.

CHAPTER SUMMARY

# What Men Can Teach Boys

### Spend time with boys

- Be interested in what interests them
- Find activities you can do together
- Give them one-on-one time
- Boys need time in the sole company of men
- Take an interest in the boys in your neighbourhood

### Be a role model

- Boys learn from everything men do
- There are some things boys can learn only from men
- Boys need to hear men tell their stories
- Encourage boys to admit when they don't know or they need help

### Guide them into manhood

- When a boy's voice breaks, it is time for men to step forward
- Find ways to welcome him into the tribe of men
- Celebrate the transition from boy to young man

NOTEBOOK

*For men:*

Which boys do you think see you or could see you as a role model?

How much time can you spend with them?
What could you do with them during this time?

If you have a son or grandson, do you have one-on-one time with him?

Are there boys in your neighbourhood who would respond to some male attention? How could you give them some?

Do you know a teenager who is in the transition from boy to young man? Could you be one of the men that guide him into manhood? Would you be prepared to? How could you do this?
[*A word of warning*: don't make any promises that you may not be able to deliver.]

*For women:*

Who can/does provide good male role models for the boys you know? What might they be able to do with those boys?

How can you help this to happen?

Can you step back and allow boys and men to spend time without you, doing their own thing in their own way?

How can you make it clear to a boy that you celebrate his transition to young man?

**About Our Boys**

# Chapter Notes

### Chapter 1  Valuing Boys and Giving Them Values

1  Dan Kindlon and Michael Thompson: *Raising Cain.*

2  John Eldredge: *Wild at Heart.*

3  Robert Bly: *Iron John.*

4  Adrienne Katz, Ann Buchanan and Anne McCoy: *Leading Lads.*

5  Adapted from a story in Jack Canfield and Mark Victor Hansen's *Chicken Soup for the Soul.*

### Chapter 2  Channelling Boys' Energy

1  Unless stated otherwise, information in this chapter referring to differences between boys' and girls' biology, behaviour or performance, and references to research, are drawn from Anne Moir and David Jessel: *BrainSex.*

2  Dan Kindlon and Michael Thompson: *Raising Cain.*

3  Steve Biddulph: *Raising Boys.*

4  Ibid.

5  Susan Seisage: *Managing an Improvement in Boys' Achievement at an Inner City College*

6  Quoted in Gwenda Sanderson: 'Being Cool and a Reader' in Rollo Browne and Richard Fletcher (eds.): *Boys in Schools.*

### Chapter 3  Boundaries and Discipline

1  'About Boys', conference organised by NCH Scotland in Glasgow, June 2003.

2  Adrienne Katz, Ann Buchanan and Anne McCoy: *Leading Lads.*

3  Ibid.

4  Vivienne Parry: *The Truth about Hormones.*

## Chapter 4  Allowing Boys to Be Their Best

1  Adrienne Katz, Ann Buchanan and Anne McCoy: *Leading Lads.*
2  Adapted from Kenneth Blanchard and Spencer Johnson's *The One Minute Manager.*

## Chapter 5  Giving Boys an Emotional Vocabulary

1  Steve Biddulph: *Raising Boys.*
2  Adrienne Katz, Ann Buchanan and Anne McCoy: *Leading Lads.*

## Chapter 6  Twelve Ways to Avoid Shouting and Nagging

1  Adele Faber and Elaine Mazlish: *How to Talk So Kids Will Listen and Listen So Kids Will Talk.*

## Chapter 7  What Men Can Teach Boys

1  Adrienne Katz, Ann Buchanan and Anne McCoy: *Leading Lads.*
2  John Eldredge: *Wild at Heart.*

# Bibliography

Teri **Apter** (2001): *The Myth of Maturity*, W.W. Norton, London

Madeleine **Arnot**, John Gray, Mary James and Jean Rudduck (1998): *Recent Research on Gender and Educational Performance* (OFSTED Reviews of Research), HMSO, London

Steve **Biddulph** (1994): *Manhood*, Hawthorn Press, Stroud

Steve **Biddulph** (1998): *Raising Boys*, Thorsons, London

Kenneth **Blanchard** and Spencer Johnson (1982): *The One Minute Manager*, Fontana, Glasgow

Robert **Bly** (1990): *Iron John*, Rider, Random House Group, London

Rollo **Browne** and Richard Fletcher (eds.) (1995): *Boys in Schools*, Finch Publishing, Sydney

N. **Browne** and C. Ross: 'Girls' Stuff, Boys' Stuff: Young Children Talking and Playing' in N. Browne (ed.) (1991): *Science and Technology in the Early Years*, Open University Press, Milton Keynes

Jack **Canfield** and Mark Victor Hansen (eds.) (1993): *Chicken Soup for the Soul: 101 Stories to Open the Heart and Rekindle the Spirit*, Health Communications, Deerfield Beach, Florida

Stephen **Covey** (1992): *Seven Habits of Highly Effective People*, Simon & Schuster, London

Paul **Dennison** (2002): *Brain Gym*, VAK Verlags, Hamburg

John **Eldredge** (2001): *Wild at Heart: Discovering the Secrets of a Man's Soul*, Thomas Nelson, Nashville

Adele **Faber** and Elaine Mazlish (1980): *How to Talk So Kids Will Listen and Listen So Kids Will Talk*, Simon & Schuster, London

Roger **Fisher** and William Ury (1981): *Getting to Yes*, Arrow Books, London

Stephen **Frosh**, Ann Phoenix and Rob Pattman (2002): *Young Masculinities*, Palgrave, Basingstoke

Daniel **Goleman** (1996): *Emotional Intelligence*, Bloomsbury, London

John **Gray** (1992): *Men Are from Mars and Women Are from Venus*, Thorsons, London

Michael **Gurian** (1996): *The Wonder of Boys*, Tarcher/Putnam, New York

Tim **Kahn** (1998): *Bringing up Boys*, Piccadilly Press, London

Adrienne **Katz**, Ann Buchanan and Anne McCoy (1999): *Leading Lads*, Young Voice, East Moseley

Dan **Kindlon** and Michael Thompson (1999): *Raising Cain*, Michael Joseph, London

Genie Z. **Laborde** (1983): *Influencing with Integrity*, Syntony Publishing, Palo Alto, California

Celia **Lashlie** (2006): *He Will Be OK: Growing Gorgeous Boys into Great Men*, Harper Collins, New Zealand

Mairtin **Mac an Ghaill** (1994): *The Making of Men: Masculinities, Sexualities and Schooling*, Open University Press, Buckingham

Dianne **McGuinness** (1985): *When Children Don't Learn*, Basic Books, New York

Anne **Moir** and David Jessel (1993): *BrainSex*, Mandarin, London

Eli H. **Newberger** (1999): *Bringing up a Boy*, Bloomsbury, London

Lennart **Nilson** (1990): *A Child Is Born*, Doubleday, London

Sue **Palmer** (2006): *Toxic Childhood*, Orion Books, London

Vivienne **Parry** (2005): *The Truth about Hormones*, Atlantic Books, London

Marshall **Rosenberg** (2003): *Nonviolent Communication – A Language for Life*, Puddledance Press, California

Gwenda **Sanderson**: 'Being Cool and a Reader' in Rollo Browne and Richard Fletcher (eds.) (1995): *Boys in Schools*, Finch Publishing, Sydney

Susan **Seisage** (2001): *Managing an Improvement in Boys' Achievement at an Inner City College*, a dissertation for the MBA in Educational Management, University of Leicester, unpublished

Robin **Skinner** and John Cleese (1993): *Families and How to Survive Them,* Vermilion, London

Barbara **Straugh** (2003): *Why Are They So Weird? What's Really Going on in a Teenager's Brain*, Bloomsbury, London

Mark **Twain** (1876): *The Adventures of Tom Sawyer*

Marian **Woodhall** (1990): *How to Talk So Men Will Listen*, Contemporary Books, Chicago

# Recommended Reading for Boys

When asked what kind of books they liked, boys said:

*Magical Books*          *Adventure Books*       *Animal Books*
*Mystery Books*          *Funny Books*           *Horror*
*Fantasy*               *Information books*      *Atlases*
*Mythical Legends*

The lists below start with books for younger readers and progress to those suitable for older readers.

**Non-Fiction**

Joke books, comics, magazines

*How* books, Usborne Publishing

*I Wonder Why* series, Kingfisher

*Eyewitness* series, Dorling Kindersley

*Observer* series, Penguin

*History Detective* series, Philip Ardagh, Macmillan Children's Books

*Horrible Histories* series, Terry Deary, Scholastic Hippo

*Adventures from History* series, Ladybird Books, Wills & Hepworth

*Horrible Science*, Nick Arnold, Scholastic

*Just Stupid*, Andy Griffiths, Macmillan Children's Books

*Explorers Wanted* series, Simon Chapman, Egmont Books

*Guinness Book of Records*, Gullane Publishing

*Coping with School*, Peter Corey, Scholastic

*Boys Behaving Badly*, Jeremy Daldry, Piccadilly Press

**Fiction**

*Elephants Don't Sit on Cars*, David Henry Wilson, Macmillan Children's Books

*Bad Boys (Strikers)*, David Ross and Bob Cattell, André Deutsch

*The Story of the Little Mole Who Knew It Was None of His Business*, Werner Holzwarth, Chrysalis Children's Books
*Prince Cinders*, Babette Cole, Puffin Books
*Horrible Henry*, Francesca Simon, Dolphin
*Greek Myths* retold by Heather Amery, Usborne Publishing
*I Wish, I Wish*, Paul Shipton, Oxford Reading Tree
*Mr Majeika*, Humphrey Carpenter, Puffin Books
*The Twits*, Roald Dahl, Puffin Books
*Viking at School*, Jeremy Strong, Puffin Books
*Goosebumps* series, R.L. Stine, Scholastic
*Football Crazy*, Patricia Borlenghi, Bloomsbury Publishing
*Short!*, Kevin Crossley, Oxford University Press
*The Bugalugs Bum Thief*, Tim Winton, Puffin Books
*Top Ten Greek Legends*, Terry Deary, Scholastic
*The Adventures of Junior James Bond*, R D Mascott, Jonathan Cape Children's Books
*Captain Underpants*, Dav Pilkey, Scholastic
*Harry Potter*, J. K. Rowling, Bloomsbury Publishing
*Mrs Frisby and the Rats from NIMH*, Robert C. O'Brien, Puffin Books
*Scary Stories to Tell in the Dark*, Alvin Schwartz, Lippincott, Williams & Wilkins
*Ghost Dog*, Eleanor Allen, Little Apple Books
*Narnia Collection*, C.S. Lewis, Puffin Books
*Hardy Boys Mystery Stories*, Franklin W. Dixon, Simon & Schuster Children's Books
*I Was a Rat*, Philip Pullman, Corgi Yearling
*Scribbleboy*, Philip Ridley, Puffin Books
*Grandma Baa*, Roger Hargreaves, Macmillan Children's Books
*The Wind Singer,* William Nicholson, Egmont Books
*Gift of the Gab*, Maurice Gleitzman, Puffin Books

*The Saga of Darren Shan*, Collins
*Feather Boy*, Nicky Singer, Collins
*The Kite Rider*, Geraldine McCaughrean, Oxford University Press
*Hydra*, Robert Swindells, Corgi Yearling
*Kensuke's Kingdom*, Michael Morpurgo, Mammoth
*Cliffhanger*, Jacqueline Wilson, Corgi Yearling
*A Series of Unfortunate Adventures*, Lemony Snicket, Egmont Books
*Swallows and Amazons*, Arthur Ransome, Red Fox
*The Number Devil*, Hans Magnus Enzensberger, Granton Books
*Point Blanc*, Anthony Horowitz, Walker Books
*Wrecked*, Robert Swindells, Puffin Books
*Holes*, Louis Sachar, Bloomsbury Publishing
*Face*, Benjamin Zephaniah, Bloomsbury Publishing
*Unbelievable*, Paul Jennings, Puffin Books
*The Phantom Tollbooth*, Norton Juster, Collins
*Horowitz Horror*, Anthony Horowitz, Orchard Books
*Street Child*, Berlie Doherty, Collins
*Scupper Hargreaves, Football Genius*, Chris d'Lacey, Corgi Yearling
*The Shadow of the Minotaur Trilogy*, Alan Gibbons, Orion Children's Books
*War Boy*, Michael Foreman, Puffin Books
*Tales of Redwall*, Brian Jaques, Philomel Books
*Worlds of Chrestimanci*, Diana Wynne Jones, Collins
*Flour Babies*, Anne Fine, Puffin Books
*Uncle Albert* series, Russell Stannard, Faber & Faber
*The Silver Sword*, Ian Seraillier, Puffin Books
*Julie and Me and Michael Owen Makes Three*, Alan Gibbons, Orion Children's Books

*The Dadhunters*, Josephine Feeney, Collins
*Artemis Fowl*, Eoin Colfer, Penguin
*Buffy the Vampire Slayer*, Nancy Holder and Christopher
Golden, Pocket Books
*His Dark Materials* trilogy, Philip Pullman, Scholastic
*Lord of the Rings*, J. R. R. Tolkien, Harper Collins

## Poetry
*Silly Verse for Kids*, Spike Milligan, Puffin Books
*The Spot on My Bum*, Gez Walsh, The King's England Press
*Please Mrs Butler*, Allan Ahlberg, Puffin Books
*Revolting Rhymes*, Roald Dahl, Puffin Books
*Big Bad Raps*, Tony Mitton, Orchard Books
*Beowulf* translated by Seamus Heaney, Penguin
*The Iron Wolf,* Ted Hughes, Faber & Faber
*Shortcuts and Teenage Ramblings*, Patrick and Tim
Chasslis, Balanced Books

## Reading Resources
www.cool-reads.co.uk
www.guysread.com
www.ukchildrensbooks.co.uk
www.lemonysnicket.com
www.darrenshan.com
www.amazon.co.uk

# Resources

## Parenting

**Fathers Direct** is the national information centre on fatherhood.
9 Nevill Street, Abergavenny NP7 5AA
**www.fathersdirect.com**
**Tel: 0845 634 1328**

**Parents Centre** is a website developed by the Department of Education and Skills for parents. It includes advice on bullying, truancy, behaviour and discipline.
**www.parentscentre.gov.uk**

**Parentline** is staffed by trained volunteers, all of whom have parenting experience. They offer information and support, and the chance to talk through the issues facing parents. Their 24-hour service is free and confidential.
**www.parentlineplus.org.uk**
**Tel: 0808 800 2222**

**Parent Network** is a national charity that offers a range of courses to parents and professionals supporting families.
Room 2, Winchester House, Kennington Park,
11 Cranmer Road, London SW9 6EJ
**Tel: 0207 735 1214**

**Raising Kids** has a website for parents of children from birth to 21 years.
117 Rosebery Road, London N10 2LD
**www.raisingkids.co.uk**
**Tel: 0208 883 8621**

## Men and Boys

**Working with Men** develops projects, initiatives and campaigns to benefit and support the development of boys, young men and adults.
Unit K, 401 Tower Bridge Business Complex, 100 Clements Road, London SE16 4DG
**www.workingwithmen.org**
**Tel/Fax: 0207 237 5353**

**National Youth Agency** supports those involved in young people's personal and social development and has a website that is an information toolkit for young people.
**www.youthinformation.com**

## Drugs Information

**Frank** provides good street-wise information about drugs for children and adults.
**www.talktofrank.com**
**Tel: 0800 77 66 00**

## Mental Health

**Young Minds** is the national charity committed to improving the mental health of all children and young people.
48-50 St John Street, London EC1M 4DG
**www.youngminds.org.uk**
**Tel: 0207 336 8445**

## Internet Safety

**Get Safe Online** is an information site for parents and young people on how to use the Internet safely.
**www.getsafeonline.org**

**About Our Boys**

# Index

If you would like to make any comments about the book or have Lucinda Neall address a group about bringing the best out in boys, please contact her at the address below:

> Neall Scott Partnership Ltd
> 4 Tornay Court
> Slapton
> Leighton Buzzard
> United Kingdom
> LU7 9DA
>
> tel:    0044 (0) 1525 222 600
> fax:    0044 (0) 1525 222 700
> email:  boys@neallscott.co.uk

Copies of *About Our Boys* can be obtained from:
www.lulu.com

Copies of *Bringing the Best Out in Boys – Communication Strategies for Teachers* can be obtained from:
www.hawthornpress.com

For further information see:
www.aboutourboys.com
www.neallscott.co.uk